Praise for
OFF T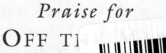

In this wonderful book, Chellis Glendinning reveals
imperialism's legacy for us all, both the children of
the oppressed and the children of the oppressor.
Off the Map is a work of great import for
our time — and it's a marvelous read, too.
— Susan Grifffin, author of *Woman and Nature*
and *A Chorus of Stones*

A stunning and unique achievement, angry and honest
and wise, which I devoured in a day and will remember for
a lifetime. It is essential for anyone who dares to figure out
what it means to be an American at this historical moment.
It is nothing less than an attempt to show the awful
consequences of the Western mindset that almost all of us
have inherited (or adopted) — what it means to be a
product of 500 years of unrelenting, violent, indefensible,
largely racist, and successful imperialism. And then
to suggest the kind of psychological transformations that
have to take place for us to understand another way of
looking at the world, and the kinds of ally we might
have for that in the people who still understand
the indigenous, tribal thoughtways.
— Kirkpatrick Sale, author of *Conquest of Paradise*
and *Rebels Against the Future*

One of the most significant books to chart the struggle between the global and the local to appear in a very long time. A dazzling contribution to the critical study of globalization (qua imperialism).
— Devon Peña, author of *Chicano Culture, Ecology, Politics: Subversive Kin*

In order to fix something, you need to know it is broken and how it got broken. Chellis Glendinning helps us see how our world was broken by empire. By revealing in poetic detail how our world was broken, Chellis provides emotional insight into how we can go about healing the world and ourselves at the same time. Some of the bravest writing I have ever enjoyed.
— Kevin Danaher, Global Exchange, author of *Ten Reasons to Abolish the IMF and the World Bank*

A powerful account of the way imperialism and the global economy shape and reshape our lives. Chellis Glendinning is an imaginative writer as well as an impressive activist for cultural preservation and environmental justice.
— Tikkun

Maps and technology. Empire and rape. Land and people. Landscape and culture. Autonomy and domination. These themes are seamlessly merged, revealed and untangled.
— Mitchell Thomashow, author of *Ecological Identity: Becoming a Reflective Environmentalist*

This shamanic journey into the imperialist mindset
brings together gritty and little-known information with
a wonderful and unique style of writing that merges
the masculine and the feminine. Powerful, at times,
shocking; the best book I've read in a decade.
— Suzi Gablik, author of
The Re-enchantment of Art, in Lapis

Glendinning's freewheeling, lyrical meditation
on the human costs of economic globalization fiercely
blends the personal and the political.
— *Publisher's Weekly*

…a wildly potent book that demands we ask ourselves:
How deeply did we buy into the colonialists' psyche?
What elements of the dominator Empire still reside in us?
We cannot console ourselves into thinking that this
empire building is from the past and that our personal
lives have not been tainted by it. Chellis reveals to
us in subtle and not so subtle ways how we are
interdependent — how what's happening to indigenous
cultures happened to us "a long time ago … only slower."
… The colonizers have become the colonized…
Read it if you have the courage.
— Bob Banner, *HopeDance* magazine

off the map

AN EXPEDITION
DEEP INTO EMPIRE AND THE
GLOBAL ECONOMY

CHELLIS GLENDINNING

NEW SOCIETY PUBLISHERS

Cataloguing in Publication Data:

A catalog record for this publication is available from the National Library of Canada.

Copyright © 2002 by Chellis Glendinning.
All rights reserved.

Cover design by Diane McIntosh. Cover image Jess Alford, ©PhotoDisc.

Printed in Canada by Friesens Inc.

Paperback ISBN: 0-86571-463-0

Inquiries regarding requests to reprint all or part of *Off The Map: An Expedition Deep into Empire and The Global Economy* should be addressed to New Society Publishers at the address below.

To order directly from the publishers, please add $4.50 shipping to the price of the first copy, and $1.00 for each additional copy (plus GST in Canada). Send check or money order to:

New Society Publishers
P.O. Box 189, Gabriola Island, BC
V0R 1X0, Canada
1-800-567-6772

New Society Publishers' mission is to publish books that contribute in fundamental ways to building an ecologically sustainable and just society, and to do so with the least possible impact on the environment, in a manner that models this vision. We are committed to doing this not just through education, but through action. We are acting on our commitment to the world's remaining ancient forests by phasing out our paper supply from ancient forests worldwide. This book is one step towards ending global deforestation and climate change. It is printed on acid-free paper that is 100% old growth forest-free (**100% post-consumer recycled**), processed chlorine free, and printed with vegetable based, low VOC inks. For further information, or to browse our full list of books and purchase securely, visit our website at: www.newsociety.com

NEW SOCIETY PUBLISHERS   www.newsociety.com

For Annie Prutzman

and Susan Griffin

Contents

Acknowledgments

I wish to express my gratitude to many people for their support in the research and writing of this book. I am especially grateful to John Raatz, who believed in the project from start to finish and in between. Heartfelt thanks go to the northern New Mexico community: Antonio DeVargas, Andrés Vargas, Elena Avila, Orlando Romero, Jaime Chavez, Mark Schiller, Kay Matthews, Georgia Roybal, Roberto Mondragón, Lilian Córdova, Hilario Romero, Michael Coca, Roberto Roibal, Antonio Rodarte, Jerry Fuentes, Mary y Orlando Martinez. Your work and friendship make life more rewarding than it has ever been. Special thanks for specific help with the book: Lorenzo Valdez, Moises Morales, Max Córdova, Manuel Trujillo, Joe Gonzales, David Córdova. Y a Jerry Padilla por tu ayuda con el dialecto norteño, mil gracias.

My colleagues at the Jacques Ellul Society have been inspirational. I'd like to name Kirkpatrick Sale, Beth Burrows, Stephanie Mills, Vandana Shiva, Charlene Spretnak, Ted Roszak, Dick Sclove, Andrew Kimbrell, and Langdon Winner.

I'd also like to give thanks to the authors who most informed my sense of language and style in this effort: Susan Griffin and A. A. Milne.

Thanks as well to Donna Henes, Jose Barerra, Marc Kasky, Claire Cummings, Annie Prutzman, Ruth Rutherford, Margo Adair, and Jo Eberl for critical input. To Bruce Richardson, Scott Pittman, and Greg Mello for cartographic intelligence. To my courageous readers: Mitch Thomashow, Laura Sewall, Craig Comstock, Birgitta Jansen-Nurmi, and Kay Matthews. Thanks to my editors, Emily Hilburn Sell at Shambhala and Chris Plant at New Society. To Justine Johnson for public relations. To the Foundation for Deep Ecology, Gene Hoffman, Andrew Beath, Carol Bernstein Ferry, and Marc Kasky for financial help. To Art and Carole Pruett at Box-Pack-Mail for kindness and typing cassettes, El Parasól por los burritos, y Darren Córdova y Calor por la música fantástica. And for general enthusiasm: Lindsay Holt II and Reina Attias. And, for giving me more than she'll ever know, Judith Plant.

Without which.

This book was written with Blackfeet Indian Earth pencils on post-consumer recycled paper.

Foreword
Empire in Denial

by Kevin Danaher

Chellis Glendinning manages an impressive feat: she takes us on an emotional roller coaster from the global economy to the inner depths of the human soul and back again. In some of the bravest writing I have ever enjoyed, she lays bare the human tissue connecting the divide-and-rule tactics of colonial empires with the splitting of the self that occurs when children are physically abused. Her own personal trauma at the hands of a cruel father has armed her with a keen ability for exposing injustice.

She returns often to the theme of maps (of all sorts) because they are how we navigate the world. When maps are structured to serve wealth and power, they lead the human race to conquest and exploitation. When they are structured by life values rather than money values, they take us to a compassionate terrain. She reminds us that "the notion of owned earth originates in maps."

In order to fix something, you need to know it is broken and how it got broken. Chellis Glendinning helps us see how our world has been broken by empire. By revealing in poetic detail how this happened, Chellis provides emotional insight into how we can go about healing the world and ourselves at the same time.

Her deft exposure of all things imperial could not come at a more appropriate time in the history of the United States. This book will speed up a process that is already underway: Americans are gradually waking up to the fact that the United States is not just a nation, it is an empire. For nearly six decades we have been the dominant military, political, economic, and cultural force on the face of the Earth.

We have a track record that can be seen as a glass-half-full or a glass-half-empty.

The glass-half-full (the view of ourselves most promoted by the corporate media and, understandably, embraced by the public) is that the United States has been a cheerleader for democracy and human rights, a protector of the weak, and a purveyor of useful goods and services. The case for this view can be found in the daily news media (especially television) and abundantly in academic literature.

For balance, we also need to consider the glass-half-empty side of the equation. During the past century, U.S. rulers have overthrown more elected governments, bombed more countries, and resisted more international human rights and environmental treaties than any other regime in the world. The American people have consumed more of the world's resources and, on a per capita basis, polluted more of the planet than any other people.

Americans did not consciously set out to be the global glutton. At the end of World War II there was only one major industrial power left standing, and that was the United States. American corporations and the U.S. military expanded into countries once dominated by Japan and the European colonial powers.

Foreign élites willing to collaborate with U.S. companies extracting wealth from their nations were handsomely rewarded with aid and access to U.S. markets. Many of these regimes developed more accountability to Washington and Wall Street than to their own people. U.S. policy makers were more concerned with economic and geostrategic issues of U.S. global power than with whether all of the children were being fed and elections were fair. The key criterion used by our leaders to determine who was "a friend of America" was the willingness of foreign élites to open their economies to U.S. companies coming in to extract human and natural wealth, not whether they supported American ideals of the inalienable rights of "life, liberty and the pursuit of happiness" and a justice system based on "the truth, whole truth, and nothing but the truth."

A consistent thread in our foreign policy has been preventing economic nationalism: all the regimes opposed by Washington — communist and noncommunist alike — have shared this characteristic: they wanted their national resources to benefit their own people rather than foreign corporations. Mossadegh in Iran, Lumumba in the Congo, Arbenz in Guatemala, and many more, were elected, noncommunist leaders who were deposed by U.S. policy makers because they were seen as a threat — not to America per se, but to the profits of large corporations. And, as Chellis Glendinning summarizes, the corporations "took away local control and made everyone dependent on their money."

The problem with the U.S. foreign policy mantra of "our-way-or-the-highway" is that it has gained us questionable "friends" in high places around the world, and a reputation for hypocrisy among the majority classes (workers, peasants, and small business people).

If U.S. élites are basing their global power on alliances with foreign undemocratic élites who are willing to collaborate in the exploitation of "their" people and "their" natural environments, then the American people need to be lied to about what is really going on, because most Americans are not conscious imperialists. They may benefit from the structure of empire but they don't like to think of their country as a global bully. The solution? The same corporations that dominate the government also dominate the public airwaves, filling the public consciousness with mind candy (commodity consciousness) rather than facts, analysis, or true emotion.

Just look at the "war on terrorism" being waged by the U.S. government. What would happen if the corporate media pursued the following questions?

- What percentage of Americans could find Afghanistan on a map? Should the citizens of America not be required to be able to locate a country on a map before we bomb that country and smash it even more than we did during our previous jihad in Afghanistan (1979-89) against the USSR?

- When the CIA was training Islamic militants during the Soviet invasion of Afghanistan, which of our public servants aided and abetted the heroin traffic being used to raise money for terrorists who were then "our" terrorists?

- Winston Churchill said, "Appeasement is thinking you can feed the crocodile and thus be the last one eaten." What agencies of the U.S. government fed this crocodile? Who raised it from a fledgling movement and trained it in weaponry and killing in the name of Allah?

- Why were so many innocent people in the U.S.A. killed or harassed following September 11 because of the way they looked?
- Why do we name our attack helicopters (Apache, Blackhawk) after peoples who suffered genocide at the hands of the invading Europeans?
- Given that America is the most diverse country in the world, why are our television sets so dominated by wealthy white males who represent the military-industrial complex that President Dwight Eisenhower warned us against?
- Why would some Americans consider the mere asking of these questions to be unpatriotic rather than patriotic?

We all need to address the big question: Shall we try to remain an empire via a "fortress America" strategy, or should we make a transition to being one nation in a community of nations? This question represents a crucial fork in the road. Maintaining empire directs us toward the unilateralist policies favored by the Bush administration and more restrictions on civil liberties at home. Benjamin Franklin said, "Those who would give up essential liberty to purchase a little temporary safety deserve neither liberty nor safety." A transition away from empire requires a more collaborative, multilateralist strategy — one that could create a more affordable approach to international security than anything that will ever come from a reliance on U.S. military force.

By focusing on the insights of indigenous cultures (as opposed to the addictive behavior of the commodity culture), Chellis Glendinning suggests that we hitch our star to the majority classes abroad rather than the collaborator élites who care more about their Swiss bank accounts than their own people. She leaves the reader convinced that a populist shift in our foreign policy would be better for the world — and it would be better for us.

Chellis exposes the core problem of our age — that our consciousness is disconnected from other forms of life, alienated from both mother and mother nature. As Michael Lerner has said, "When the understanding of our interconnection is lost, people start to proceed in a way that is analogous to the misunderstanding that happens with a cancer cell. The cancer cell, the cell that pays attention to its own interest without regard to the other cells around it, starts to consume more and more and more. So it's not surprising that cancer really is the quintessential sickness of the contemporary age."

Healing for us as individuals is dependent on the larger global project of reconnecting all the broken pieces of the web of life back into a harmonious whole. The good news is that there is a growing international movement to fully democratize the planet, from the grassroots up. The paradigm of money values/violence/God-is-on-my-side is steadily losing public support to the ascendant paradigm of life values/nonviolence/God-does-not-take-sides-in-intraspecies-conflicts.

This paradigm shift is the first truly global revolution. Previous revolutions were national in scope; they sought control over the capital city. But notice that when the Zapatistas rose up in Chiapas in 1994, they did not say they wanted to seize power in Mexico City. They rose up against the neoliberal economic model (in the form of NAFTA, the IMF and the World Bank) that was — and is — cutting down their forests and starving their children.

The global-values revolution is crossing all national and institutional boundaries for the simple reason that, as both the social crisis of inequality and the environmental crisis get steadily worse, more and more people are finding it harder to ignore the emergency confronting us.

Chellis Glendinning's search for a new direction — a life-affirming, justice-seeking direction — could not be more timely. Our age is in desperate need of healing: that is the "big job" confronting us. Chellis prepares us for that job by giving us guideposts for linking our spiritual lives with the fate of all life. If we can accomplish that, there is still hope for saving the human race from itself.

Kevin Danaher is a co-founder of the international human rights organization Global Exchange. His most recent book is *Ten Reasons to Abolish the IMF and the World Bank.*

LOCATION UNKNOWN

The best of all Good Companions to take with you to a
strange place is undoubtedly A MAP.

— Walter W. Jervis, *The World in Maps*

The orange-vested surveyor is searching for a United States Bureau of Land Management brass cap from which to locate his calculations. He must document exactly, to the yucca blade, where the pasture ends and Vigil's weeds begin. This land of northern New Mexico may appear to be made of wildly loping badlands, sand-pink barrancas that give not a wisp of wind for human affairs, and crazy fences sculpted from rusting bedsprings and World War II missile shells. But down at the capital, the land is measured to precision.

On the Public Lands Survey, the piñons and rabbit holes are divided and subdivided into checkerboards of townships and ranges, segmented and subsegmented to numerical exactitude, and registered as real estate. According to the international Latin-Long system, these arroyos and olive stands reside as a tight grid of parallels and meridians calculated in the days of tall ships by the stars, now by satellite and computer, and cast onto a projection of the planet. In military cyberspace, the place is figured and refigured on the Universal Transverse Mercator, invented in 1972 when United States satellites threw orbital scan lines onto the Earth's body and called them cartography.

(Snowflake Martinez and Chellis Glendinning meet at the Public Lands Survey intersection between South 2 and 3, Township 20 North and Range 9 East. According to Latin-Long, we meet at 35 degrees 58 minutes 45 seconds north and 105 degrees 58 minutes west. We tip our hats to each other within Universal Transverse Mercator Zone 13 North at 3,983,561 meters northing and 413,047 meters easting.

You could also say that the location of our meeting lies between the Jemez Mountains on the western horizon, the Sangre de Cristos to the east, and the Rockies to the north. The desert valley in between envelops us like a tapestry patterned by coyote trails and juniper bushes. Millions of winters ago the land lay beneath a sea that, as it slowly receded, carved out valleys and gorges against the granite bedrock and these eerie pinnacles of pink sand. A volcano erupted, hurling lava bursts like water beads on wool. And then a giant stream of water flowed down from the north, twining like thread between the mountains. Along the way, smaller streams were woven in. One of them, bordering the desert just north of our meeting place, is luxuriantly hemmed by cottonwoods, willows, a slender braid of chile farms, and the village where Snowflake Martinez and I find ourselves to be neighbors.

I squint at Snowflake through the early-morning sun. His scraggly straw cowboy hat shades a clipped mustache, and his long legs are covered by tattered buckskin chaps cut in elk-button curves from hip to ankle.

"You are going to tell me about your grandmother, ¿qué no?" he asks, reining his sorrel almost parallel to the pinto mare I am riding. "You said you want to." He speaks English as if he were plucking a guitar.

I shift my weight in the stirrups, and my old saddle squeaks leather. I am almost silenced by the twisted history that separates me — European American, in these parts called "Anglo" — from this Chicano vaquero — part Mexicano, part Pueblo, part Hispano. Yet we both, with open hearts, want to understand the distance that lies between us.

"I loved my grandmother," I whisper into the desert air. "We called her Mimere."

"¿Por qué?" He leans forward to stroke his sorrel's mane.

"In French it means 'grandmother.' But further back, in legend, Mimir was the giant guarding the Well of Remembrance. *Mimir* means 'memory.'"

I look at Snowflake carefully. A bright orange bandana encircles his neck. Its intensity makes the crevasses on his face appear all the more certain.

"Mimere wore perfume every day of her life, Chanel No. 5. She and Pipere lived a grand life. That's the word they used to describe it: *grand*. They lived through the Great War, the Crash, FDR, Bing Crosby." I draw an airy pyramid against the blue sky. "My grandparents weren't on the top. They were the next rung down, the lawyers and doctors who served the top."

"¿Y la casa?"

"It was a brick house. It had an acre of rose garden out back and another acre of vegetable garden. We kids caught fireflies by the corn. We glued the lit parts onto our fingers and called them diamond rings. . . . The house was packed. Oriental rugs, Victorian couches, Chinese tea sets. I think the upstairs had four bedrooms, plus a sewing room and a plant room. What I remember best is how orderly everything was. The linens, they were so pressed, so . . . so white. Snowflake, is this *unbelievable?*"

"Sí, sí," he ponders. His horse clops iron against the sand. "This is unbelievable."

"The third floor had a playroom and a costume closet," I continue. "I loved the costumes. Especially the gold buttons on my great-grandfather's Spanish-American War uniform. There were fairy costumes, too. . . and up on the third floor was the maid's quarters."

"¿ . . . the *maid's* quarters?" Snowflake leans into his saddle horn; his eyes laser through me. "Díme," he coaxes.

". . . Irene and Helmut. They were refugees from Eastern Europe. I'm sorry, I don't remember. They didn't speak English. She was the cook; he was the gardener."

For a long moment the voice of the wind envelops us.

"I love a story," he offers kindly, and yet our bones are certain that these memories utter far more than stories can tell.

"The mother of my mother, mi abuela," he begins. I can tell by the flattened tone of his voice, by the haunted stare toward the Sangres in the distance, Snowflake is digging deep. "Mi abuela, she lived with us in the village. She smelled of herbs y wore a black wool dress that she sewed herself. Except the buttons, they were mail-order. They came by packhorse. . . . My people, eran gente de la tierra. They lived on the land in México. They lived on the land in España. They lived on the land in this valley. Mis abuelos, they saw the Revolución Mexicana y the Bataan Death March. Pero mostly they saw snowstorms y elk hunting y childbirth. . . . Mi abuela, she wore that dress to scrub, to pray, to carry her babies. She had nine babies."

I sit in the saddle utterly still.

"And the house?"

"La casa era hecha de la tierra. Había solamente un cuarto, one room. . . . One Saturday, mi abuela, she asked la gringa from the river to come by. There were chores. Mi abuela washed her dress y all our shirts. She started early that morning firing up the stove to make tortillas. There was respect in those days, ¿qué no? 'Shake hands,' she told us. 'Use the formal *usted.*' Pero la gringa talked some strange garbled language. Even if we did say 'usted,' she wouldn't know. Al fin, when the wagon rolled up the road y she climbed out, I got so scared I just stood there all staring with my big eyes. Then I ran into the outhouse, y I hid there in the heat. They called, pero I didn't make a noise until the lady went away. . . . Mis abuelos no tenían mucho, unos borregos, a wagon. Hell, we were just Mexicanos. We were on the bottom."

A brittle tumbleweed silently bounces past us. Here at this intersection of sun and wind, I sense the presence of forces beyond our grasp, forces greater than even our hearts can speak. How can it be that Snowflake Martinez and I have come from such distant histories to cross paths in this desert? Or perhaps better put, what is this unsettling gulf that makes it so miraculous for two human beings to gaze luminous into each other's souls?)

In the long-ago days when people journeyed across the land as nomads, when there were no kingdoms and no slaves, no wealth and no poverty, both my ancestors and those of Snowflake Martinez passed from one world to another just as the moon waxed and waned. Glaciers ascended only to melt away, the wind constantly shifted its voice, birds changed shape, humans moved on. Our maps were made of drawings in the sand, of rocks along the way, of songs that sang of the intertwining of place with event. And when our relations came upon an unknown band of fellow humans, they approached knowing that the basic patterns of life would be as they knew them, that only the day-to-day details might stir discomfort.

There is something terminally discomforting about this gulf I describe. Would that Snowflake and I had come from distant bands of people to meet surreptitiously at the edge of the hunting ground. In fact, what separates us is a different grasp of the deep patterns governing human community. I am of the empire world, he of the conquered. That we have met at all, that we have spoken and journeyed together, these events become miracles on the map of empire.

Arab-American cultural critic Edward Said may have said it best, and for this I am grateful: the historical experience of empire is the defining dynamic of the contemporary world.[1] It is common to every one of us, having come down through our parents and grandparents and their mothers and fathers before them, having impacted French and Algerian, Portuguese and Angolan, Spanish and Mapuche, Japanese and Manchurian, English and Lakota. Empire defines the human experience today, laying brittle itineraries that point toward predetermined journeys and not others, offering access to certain terrains and not others, mapping Snowflake's life and mapping mine.

The intersection we share offers a rare reflection. Where have we been? Where are we now? Where might we go? Of these things I speak. And yet, please be attentive: I am not here to expound upon the journeys of those who have struggled under the crushing wheel of empire, for these souls began speaking out on the first day of imperialism, and they have spoken every day since. I am here to speak about the journeys of those of us who are riding in the coach, perhaps in the front seat or in the back. I am here to talk about the relentless mappings that isolate us from our own humanity. I am here to talk empire.

Holy Roman. Ottoman. Imperial China. We have heard of these things. White man's burden. La missión civilizatrice. Manifest destiny. Noblesse oblige. Long live the Queen! We have known these things on the pages of our books, in our pageantry, in our blood. The sun never sets. Possessions, colonies, gold-gilded entranceways, velvet cloaks. These things weave through our vision; they seem natural to us. America is number one. These things are not of the past; they are here today. English only, human genome, safe for democracy. New world order. "What exactly can the world's most powerful and expandable PC do? . . . *Anything it wants*."[2]

"At some very basic level," writes Said, "imperialism means thinking about, settling on, controlling land that you do not possess, that is distant, that is lived on and owned by others."[3] Throughout history, the maps charting this effort have been crafted by the nation-state with its clutch of conquered terrains and monolithic rule. To conduct imperialism required the military force, bureaucratic organization, and psychosocial persuasion that the nation-state could muster, and together these forces contributed to and bolstered empire's most crucial internal attributes: the blinding of sight, the disjuncture of care.

To carry forth these dislocations today is a fresh proposition. Today's rendition of empire is a global affair — charted after World War II by a cabal of corporate executives, bankers, and government officials; launched by fresh regulations fostering expansionism, access to resources, and lack of accountability; insured by long-accepted practices of militarism. Today's empire is no longer dependent upon the direct usurpation of land. Instead, conquered peoples are granted the trappings of sovereignty within their homelands while their animal-brothers and plant-friends, the minerals of the land and the work of their backs, all are grabbed up and sold off by financial forces beyond their control. Today's empire is only facilitated by nation-states; it is conducted by transnational corporations. Today's empire is the global economy.

General Agreement on Tariffs and Trade. Exxon. Viacom. Fair Trade Area of the Americas. We know little about these things. Matsushita. Maastricht. Multilateral Agreement on Investments. We are learning about them.

I have heard a story about a Cambodian man who lost his ability to place himself on a map. YOU ARE HERE, the map would say. He was certain he was not.

The man had been teaching at the university, outspoken about his people's proud accomplishment of decolonization. He had worked hard all his life, his itinerary taking him from a hut at the edge of the jungle to this wooden podium — when suddenly men in laced combat boots burst into the classroom, blindfolded him with stinking rags, shoved him into the back of a truck.

He awoke in the jungle. They angled a submachine gun at his sweating temple. He bent over to clear wet vines for his captors; he planted rice. Then, led by submachine guns and followed by submachines guns, he trudged exhausted from unknown camp to unknown camp. He saw little, but he did see that the underbrush was strewn with the decaying corpses of his countrymen. The man was silent. He pretended to know nothing of words or places.

He lived.

Today the man is teaching in the university again, but he is now incapable of reading a map or locating himself in space. "It is Lam Huu again," his wife is forever saying when the phone rings. "He is at a bus station somewhere. He doesn't know where he is."

You and I, we too find ourselves at an unknown location: we are lost on the freeway, lost in language and calculations, lost to our own histories, lost on the map. Certainly, we have been made aware of the vagaries of the colonized, although sadly not through our own emergent curiosities or any fervent need to rekindle our humanity. We have been made aware of the horrors, the bloodshed, and bitterness through the irrepressible courage of the colonized. For those of us who have lived our days within the imperial world, and particularly for those of us who come from the currently most active dominating peoples, the "white race," the untested challenge is to map our place within the imperial dynamic. It is to grasp how this way of functioning damages everyone in its path, including ourselves.

As with Lam Huu, the problem of locating ourselves is a problem caused by trauma and dislocation: in our case, millennia-old dislocations of sight and care that are impressed upon us as children, that are validated by the daily ways of our world, that we carry like secret burdens every day of our lives. When called upon to locate our place on the map of empire, we immediately spill over with all the reasons why *not* to locate ourselves on the map. It would hurt, we protest. The iron-heavy veils are too ponderous to lift. The histories are too long forgotten to excavate, the confessions too excruciating to make, the revelations too disembodied to draw forth.

Yet as the colonized peoples of the world are crying out with increasing strength and conviction, a realization bursts from our hearts: if we are to become fully human, to embark upon these liftings and these excavations, these confessions and these revelations, is to lay the ground for meeting the other people of this Earth and together, at last, to join in charting a future for us all.

EMPIRE AS MAP

. . . by which land and people are put to use completely.

— Edward Said, *Culture and Imperialism*

THE MAP

Now nothing of this place is unknown.
— Susan Griffin, *Woman and Nature*

Spectator, spectacle, specimen!
— Robert Romanyshyn, *Technology as Symptom and Dream*

Empire originates in the perception of place. Maps are the tools of perception, charting land, sea, and sky — just as they map our imaginations.

The very first map I study is an immense depiction, painted during World War II, that leans up against the playroom wall. It is a children's map, and I am a child. In it the land of North America is colored a faded mustard-yellow. Festooned upon its plains and mountains are tiny sheaves of wheat, little steel mills puffing plumes of smoke, miniature ears of corn, cows spotted black and white. Amid rows of orange trees, southern California sports a Mickey Mouse–eared movie camera. The map is a child's paradise, very much like Robert Louis Stevenson's Land of Counterpane, like a dollhouse empire.

I sit, accompanied by my Winnie-the-Pooh books, and I trace my finger from the bucktooth beaver above the Great Lakes, south through the oil wells in Oklahoma, to leaping silver tarpon off the

Gulf Coast. The map tells me how to regard things. The world is a magical place, it pronounces, producing all the resources we Americans need: oil for our cars springs from the horsetail and ferns crushed into the earth millions of years ago; the sky is an infinite blue repository inhaling the fumes of our manufacture; the jungles of South America offer up rubber for our tires; good neighbor Canada gives us hardwood for our houses; milk from Iowa cows miraculously lands in glass bottles on the back stoop in Cleveland.

The grown-ups tell me that this map shows the land as it is. I have since pored over completely different depictions revealing an "America" roughly divided among native peoples who hunt buffalo, plant corn, gather berries and medicines, travel from one terrain to another on foot and, some would say, by horse. Made of buckskin, bark, and rock, these maps survive today in museums and along hiking trails. They are depictions not of ownership and consumption but of experience. To native peoples, the features of geography are perceived and interpreted through history, tradition, and kin; in relationship with the animal and plant worlds; in union with the ancestors and spirits. Maps act as springboards for storytelling, song, and ceremony concerning the human experience within the natural landscape.

The mustard-yellow nation in the playroom is different. It imprints the template for a world I am supposed to see but thankfully — for it would be too painful — not experience. It works like a charm. As the mighty U.S. of A. is busy pocketing the world's raw materials at bargain-basement prices and dishing out oil, steel, wheat, and Hollywood from the penthouse, I nurse a childlike sense that all of history has led up to this ideal and immutable 1950s moment.

Here to there: *scale and distance*. The map construes the space.

I sketch and paint with a passion. I doodle on the margin of my school assignments at every opportunity. But my delight takes the plunge to terra incognita one day in junior high school when Mrs. Froelich lines us up in the art room and insists that, from this day forward, we organize every one of our drawings according to the mathematical dictates of linear perspective. Across the hall Mr. Cronkite is at the blackboard copying triangles and cubes and instructing us to reproduce them on grid paper in our notebooks. Mr. Schneiderman is outlining western political expansion in social studies, while Miss McPhee arranges our effervescent little teenage bodies into military formation in the gymnasium. I am receiving not just an education but an education designed to reproduce in me the perception, thinking, and body language of a citizen of empire.

Linear perspective: this is the artist's invention. In it, the artist is bound to one place like a chair bolted to the floor. Encrusted in his furniture, he becomes the spectator, always observing, ever sedentary, no longer pulsing to Creation's rhythms. Look here. A medieval artist is perched, frozen, in his stone room gazing at the world through a closed window. He duplicates everything he sees through the window on his drawing board. The panes of the window impose a precise geometric grid over the world. The window frames what is outside into a never-changing object, and the artist's place behind the frame eliminates all sensual intake except vision, removing him from the smell of spring flowers and horse manure, the crumble of dirt beneath his slipper. Land and sky become his object: reduced, fragmented, vanishing into the distance; he, their spectator: estranged, immobilized, diminished.[1]

Long mile. Mean mile. Bird's-eye view. *Distance to scale: 1:1,000,000.* Medieval Europe is an era for "firsts." Mapmaking is the exciting new field. Scientific thought is invented, flourishes, is written down word by word, page by page, replacing what is left of the communal land-based philosophies that have propelled European peoples since the beginning of time. Both cartography and science share a commitment to distance: in both, the spectator views the world from far away. Both attend to scale: the world, now small, becomes information; the viewer, purportedly large, becomes the authority for interpreting it. In this same period of time, a passion to explore foreign lands erupts: the spectator acts out the insecurity of his displacement from life. Autobiography and self-portraiture become celebrated art forms: the viewer, so disconnected and so diminished, focuses on himself.[2]

In 1569 Flemish cartographer Gerardus Mercator publishes the first world map, proposing the revolutionary notion that navigators wanting to get from here to there travel *in a straight line*. "If you wish to sail from one port to another," he announces, "here is a chart, and a straight line on it, and if you follow this line carefully you will certainly arrive at your destination."[3]

Mercator accomplishes his feat of mental agility by graphing lines, running north-south east-west at right angles to each other, in a precise grid that segments the world into rectangles. The accomplishment is heralded as a major advance for European exploration. This is the navigator's invention, giving sailors and explorers a fixed system from which to figure straight-line courses.

The invention hangs in every classroom in my school. Yet the Mercator map is not true. It hangs there with its thin black lines north-south east-west, proclaiming that it is. "Ah, the world!" our little minds sing in response to the certainty of its placement on the wall. Ah, the world!

But the scale is all wrong.

The blunder comes from the difference between how things are in reality and how they appear on a flat piece of paper. On a globe, the North Pole is a point. On a wall map, it extends across the whole topside of the page. Things start off well. The scale at the equator is accurate enough, and indeed, the map is at its best within 15 degrees of the famed midline. But then everything goes awry. The farther you navigate from the equator, the stranger it gets. Mercator must stretch and tug his planet to impose a straight-line grid onto a page that can be reproduced by the new printing presses. He wrenches apart his meridians, his north-south longitude lines, until they appear equidistant from each other. But for every microspace he nudges them apart, he must divert the east-west latitude circles. He pushes and strains each little box of territory, and then he moves over and does it again. Until the rectangles in the north become taller and taller and taller while displaying no more terrain. Until 80 degrees of latitude, in the cold Arctic, appears thirty-six times its actual size.

The adaptation has curious perceptual ramifications. The tiny nations of Europe end up appearing far more substantial than they really are. The United States looks bigger than Brazil when, in fact,

Brazil is larger. Denmark's Greenland looks the same size as South America despite the fact that the southern continent (with its burgeoning population of natives) is nine times bigger.

(Snowflake calls me from a bluff above the lower trail my pinto and I have embarked upon. I look up to see him astride his dark sorrel. The wind has picked up into a midmorning swirl, and it whips Snowflake's black ponytail over his Levi collar. "¡That arroyo!" he calls to me. "Mira. It goes in the wrong direction. ¡Ven pa'cá!"

"Fine," I think. "I can get to where you are. I can do that." Without deliberation, I spur my pinto in a straight line toward Snowflake. The horse takes three steps . . . and then freezes. We stand hoof-to-hoof with a deep crevasse gouged into the bedrock, an impediment impossible to navigate. Embarrassed by my lack of foresight, I yank the reins in retreat and trace a labyrinthian path around hills, through arroyos, and up to the bluff.

"Snowflake?" I ask, trying to locate the lesson. The wind is still stirring our hair and the tumbleweeds around us. "I read a magazine article."

"Pues, díme. I don't read so much."

I rein my pinto so I am seated right next to him. "It's about these people in the South Pacific. They live on islands, and they use canoes to fish and gather shellfish and visit their relatives. But you know what? They don't have maps like ours. They have these maps made out of palm leaves and cowrie shells. The maps aren't about roads or countries or anything like that. They're about the wind."

"¿De veras?" His interest is piqued.

"But they never take the maps with them. They memorize them. And when they go to sea, they lie down in their canoes, they put their bodies against the timber, and they feel the wind and the waves with their bones."

"Sí, bueno." He is excited now.

"Snowflake? You don't use a map."

"This is correct."

"I notice that when you start out, you scan the land. Then you take off. You go this way and that, around this barranca, avoiding that arroyo, and finally you get to where you are going. Snowflake, how do you do that? It's like you *feel* the land and then you seem to know how to move with it."

"You are right," he wonders. "How you say it is how it is."

"Well, how do you do this?"

The sorrel's flank heaves a dramatic sigh, and Snowflake's black eyes turn inward to search out an explanation for something he has been doing all his life. Finally he leans across the saddle and he whispers: "For this, I find no words.")

North south east west: *direction*. The map lays the way.

After I pore over the mustard-yellow nation in the playroom, a miscellany of maps passes through my hands. There are those Triple-A TripTiks that fall across my mother's lap in the front seat of the Ford. There are maps tacked onto schoolroom bulletin boards brightly starred with the state capitals: Salem, Oregon; Harrisburg, Pennsylvania. I push these to the just-barely-awake edge of my mind. It is not until the cartographic sweep of the age of European empire makes itself known that I again take notice.

This occurs in Mr. Schneiderman's seventh-grade social studies class. I have already debased myself with the only C minus of my academic career: a torturously handmade papier-mâché rendition of my ancestors' homeland. Unfortunately, my Scottish Highlands are peaking toward the bonnie-blue sky where the Lowlands should be, and the Lowlands are slouching like lowriders where hills should be dusting the clouds. Before the study of papier-mâché cartography gives way to the not-unrelated field of European political history, there is one more class project I remember, although it is not ours. This project has been saved for the more advanced ninth grade. It is a study of propaganda. Mr. S. holds up his favorite term paper: a neatly ballpoint-penned report on the subject at hand — blown to illegible shreds by a huge, messy bullet hole.

My first critical thought in the realm of scholarship follows. Mr. S. unfurls a chart across the blackboard revealing the full achievement of European imperialism, circa 1914. It is vast. England's territory alone covers a full quarter of the globe: from Ireland, across

Africa and the Middle East, including parts of China, New Zealand, Australia, Ceylon, islands in the Caribbean, and the Indian subcontinent in its entirety — all frosted by the obligatory pink of the royal dominion. France's holdings are likewise considerable, as are those of Italy, the Netherlands, Belgium, Portugal, Germany, Russia, and the United States. Mr. S. announces with pride that the "rise of the West" constitutes the most astounding accumulation of land and resources in world history. In the year 1800, he says, Western powers hold 35 percent of the Earth's surface. By 1875, the proportion reaches 65 percent, and by 1914, the West holds a grand total of *85 percent of the Earth.*

Just over a generation later, seventh graders sit quiescent in classrooms across the United States with huge and messy bullet holes shot through our heads. European empire? This is how it is, was, and should have been. As I impatiently fidget at my writing desk, a thought wings its way into my mind like the first robin of spring. European empire? Wouldn't the very act of charting a map serve the conquerors to subjugate the land? In fact, they couldn't do it any other way — that is, *if they didn't know where they were going or where they had been.*

To-the-death races to chart where they are going and where they have been mark the age of European empire. 1857: Richard Francis Burton leads the British Royal Geographical Society's expedition to capture the headwaters of Africa's Nile River. Bolstered in the effort by more than one hundred African porters, the explorer sets out from Zanzibar to become the first European to set eyes upon the watery expanse of Lake Tanganyika. With knee-jerk alacrity, he determines this pool to be the very source the society seeks, inks it onto his charts as the official headwater of the Nile, and then, jungle fever having gotten the better of him, plunges into his cot like a bag of rocks.

The ever-ambitious John Speke then sneaks out of the encampment on his own and stumbles upon an even larger lake to the east. He names it after Queen Victoria and, with bravado, proclaims it to be the *real* fountainhead of the Nile.

Come 1864, the candelabras illuminating one of Britain's most renowned lecture halls are polished in preparation; Anglicans in their wool overcoats are lining up to hear the details of this latest cartographic spat. The day before the debate, Speke is found shot with his own hunting rifle. It is suspected that he has ended his life rather than face ridicule of his cartographic claim to fame.

Ever earnest, the society now persuades the most celebrated explorer of the century to take up the cause. David Livingstone sets out . . . and promptly disappears. Worried for its investment, the society dispatches a young newspaper reporter to track him down. Henry Stanley locates a delirious Livingstone on the eastern shore of Tanganyika. He hunches into the musty tent. "Dr. Livingstone, I presume?" Between dry coughs and nauseous swoons, Livingstone answers with the big plan: the source of the Nile lies farther south than either Burton or Speke has proposed, he wheezes. Another river, the Lualaba, must surely be the source of the Nile. But before he can track this uncharted river, Livingstone keels over, slumped on his knees as if in prayer, dead as a dog. Devotedly, his native helpers carve out his entrails and bury them under a tree. The body then makes its final voyage to the motherland to be interred beneath the marble floors at Westminster Abbey.

Henry Stanley settles the mystery of the Nile. Equipped with a humongous barge, he traces the Kagera River southwest from Lake Victoria to the Nile's first tender tricklings in the Burundi mountains. He sets off again, this time accompanied by seven hundred porters, to chart the unknown Lualaba, which Livingstone has proposed to be the fountainhead of the Nile. He endures constant attack from angry tribes and loses hundreds of men to disease and starvation. But Stanley is nothing if not determined; he discovers once and for all that the Lualaba holds no relation to the Nile.

In a mere three years, Henry Stanley surpasses all previous explorers in the effort to commit Africa to parchment. Along the way, he cannot help making diplomatic headway as well. His accomplishments open the terrain not just to European-style cartographic abstraction but to European-style settlement; European-style roads and railways; European-style exploitation of animals, plants, minerals, and peoples; European-style government. Stanley tricks the

Bugandan people at the north end of Lake Victoria into hosting a Christian mission, a foothold that leads to the founding of the British protectorate of Uganda. Undaunted by considerations of national loyalty, he goes on to establish trading posts up and down the Congo River for Leopold's Belgian "kingdom."

(We come upon a trickling of a desert river. We dismount. Snowflake unsheathes a crude knife with a leather handle. I take out my Swiss Army, and without talking we trail both sides of the stream, cutting bouquets of the purple-flowered trébol herb. When we each accumulate a delicate collection, we meet back by the horses. Silently we place our flowers on the grass; we kick off our boots. Our toes brush the sand like the cheek-feather kiss of a flicker bird.

"To me it is pleasing to be here," confesses Snowflake. "Here, este río. I was here before con mi abuelo on our way up the monte to hunt. We were riding burros, not horses como now. Mira."

He is pointing to a granite boulder in the grass. Oh. I see. It has a picture etched onto its rock marrow. The picture is a human hand. Snowflake places his hand over the image. It makes a perfect fit.

"When mis antepasados ran away from the Apaches, they stopped by this little río to get water. They were afraid for their lives, ¿qué no?"

"What does the hand mean?"

"Pa' mí, es la mano de Dios, the hand of God. Have faith, it is saying." He clasps his own hands in his lap, breathes quietly, and then turns to me as if to deliver a message. "I have been to México y Califas in my life. Also Texas y Colorado," he says. "Pero I have not much desire to go anymore." He edges over to the flowing water and mindfully lowers one foot into the stream. "I want only to be here, to be in love with *this* land.")

This and that: *detail*. The map names what is.

A tradition gets started in the early years of junior high. On a Friday night, usually in November, a chattering coterie of girls assembles in my mother's kitchen, overflowing with butter and

molasses, to execute a gingerbread map of the United States. The
execution is massive. And detailed. We construct each section of the
country on a separate baking tin — contouring the Rocky
Mountains in dough, painting the Finger Lakes with blue food col-
oring, marking the forests of the Northwest in green sprinkles, the
state capitals with silver balls. We bake each section at 375 degrees
and then assemble them all into one steaming jigsaw masterpiece on
the dining room table. The result is a teenage triumph, fraught with
hysterical tittering — and almost no hands-on living-breathing
knowledge of the terrain we are charting.

For our homey project, who could care? We bake our gingerbread
U.S.A. for fun. Yet as we giggle, unbeknownst to ourselves, we are
learning an axiom of imperialist cartography: the mapmaker is
omnipresent. He comes from elsewhere nowhere everywhere, hauling in the tools of calculation — parchment and plume; measuring
wheel and astrolabe; surveyor's level, chain, and brass caps; helicop-
ter, satellite, return-beam vidicon, four-channel multispectral scanner. All the while, the living details of the place, the details that
chronicle the daily intimacy of people with place — how they make
their way, when the elk sip at the pool, where the tadpoles wriggle
and grow, how the cottonwoods breathe into the wind — these
details are missed and dismissed. They fall into oblivion, and only the
details of the imperial fiat remain.

From this perspective, waterways are details of great import.
European exploration is fueled by a drive to obtain resources from
faraway peoples and faraway places — and one must get there if one
is to get the goods. The British Empire gets the goods. One detail is
not well understood: England could never have accomplished the
feat of capital accumulation, technological development, and mass-
scale manufacture that historians call the industrial revolution without the dirt cheap materials and labor it wrenched from India. This
fact is overlooked in common parlance, while only the wonder of the
accomplishment is touted. Machines! Factories! Finery! Yet, indeed,
how could a nation catapult its production so far beyond what it has
within its own shores *without access to other shores*?

Detail: England explodes, India implodes. The British East India
Company sets up its first textile factory along the Mahanadi River in

the state of Bengal. The year is 1633. In return for monies slipped to the governor, the company receives rights to a "free trade" that, in fact, gives it freedom while taking freedom away from indigenous weavers and merchants. Exemption from taxation is the first such right. Next, Bengal's weavers are forbidden to work for themselves. Then, factory-made textiles are priced to undercut what local weavers charge to make a profit. Finally, the company receives the right to stop Indian merchants attempting their own trade.

On the Dutch East India Company's 1648 map, "Nova totius Terrarum Orbis Tabula," the Mahanadi River is designated a prominent detail.

Details, details. Terrain on a map displaying no detail at all presents mortal embarrassment to the cartographer. "It was almost a religious duty not to leave a blank," writes geographer Walter Jervis, "a sign of abysmal ignorance."[4] One of the most amusing attempts to avoid the display of ignorance is a calligraphy legend filling in a roaring blank on a medieval mappae mundi of northeast Asia: "Hinc Abundant Leones," it trumpets, Here Lions Abound.

Detail: the empire turns on itself. It always has. The blatant turning against the people and land in faraway places mirrors the same turning within the empire itself. Hinc Abundant Leones. The year is 1770. Lancashire County, England, heartland of Britain, where tales of the infamous Robin Hood still pass from mother to daughter by the cackling hearth. Find it on the map. Life here is good. The weaver is working in his stone cottage. His little ones play as they clean the weft; the weaver's wife cards and spins. The older girls hoe their vegetable garden and walk about the village, gossiping and showing their skirts. The weaver climbs onto his roof to repair the thatching. His family is growing their own carrots and herbs, raising chickens and turkeys, earning twenty shillings a week.

The year is 1820. Lancashire County. The empire turns on itself. Life is no longer good. In a single generation the land has been made unrecognizable by the assault of industrialism. The houses, now better described as hovels, are blackened by smoke belching from six-storey textile factories. Gardens are dry from neglect and overrun by char-faced vagrants. Just as in India, the local weavers are outtaxed, and the lower prices of factory-made goods force them to give up.

They labor now sixteen hours a day at machines that dictate the pace in filthy little rooms, earning five shillings a week. For any spinner found with his window open, the penalty is one shilling. For a spinner late to his machine, two shillings.[5] Everything seems lost. The community is broken. The weaver's children are strapped to their stations with hemp, and the foreman stomps down the aisles using a leather piece to whip those who are slumped over, hysterical with fear, or numb with boredom. Sometimes he hauls a child out back by the trash bins and rapes him in the anus.

("¿Che?" Now both of Snowflake's feet, looking brown and pink like river trout, are bobbing in the water. "¿Che, what of tus padres?"

"I like to talk about my grandmother, Snowflake. I don't like to talk about my parents."

This statement strikes Snowflake as unbelievable. "¿Por qué no?" he gasps.

"My father was not a nice man."

"¿He was strict?" Such a quality is apparently the worst he can imagine.

"Worse than that." The facts of history do not lend themselves to the songs of the river. My bones quiver in expectation of the rejection I sense will come if I tell him. "He raped and beat me and my brother."

"¡Oh, Che!" Without repulsion or judgment, Snowflake grasps my grass-stained hand and presses it to his cheek. "Del mero fondo de mi corazón, I am sorry. So sorry.")

The people are changed. The land is changed. The mapmaker himself is changed. The map does not show the changes.

ROUTES AND ROADS

With the arrival of the white man came the roads.

— Letter from the indigenous people of the Pantanel to the
International Development Bank, 1996

The landscape will never be the same.

— Jeep advertisement, 1998

To the European mind, the etching of routes and roads onto
maps makes certain returning to a desirable place. Find it on
paper; get your colonels, bureaucrats, and men of the cloth there in
person. To the imperial mind, charted trails and thoroughfares
become announcements of possibility, invitations to invasion.

At the start of the European mapmaking endeavor, though, roads
are not important details to display. The vast expanses of foreign terrain measured and documented are, after all, traversed only by locals.
As it becomes apparent that roads will be necessary for empire, roads
make their appearance on parchment and, eventually, become central to the mapped imagination.

The first road map is carved onto wood within Europe itself:
"Der Rom Weg," circa 1500. It delineates the trade routes leading
to the Roman metropolis from Denmark north and Naples south,
from Paris west and Cracow east, with three passages across the
treacherous Alps. Unlike the lateral travel-and-exchange engaged in

by native peoples, this new kind of trade is in the business of expanding its sphere — expanding, ever expanding, high and low, into a worldly dominion. Roads. Arteries. Boulevards. They make it happen. Silk Road. They cut through raw terrain, defining an unprecedented march. Santa Fe Trail. El Camino Real. They belch soot into sweet air. Union Pacific. Oriental Express. They echo the hard flap of canvas against wood, throw billows of blackened steam into the sky. Northwest Passage. Roads. Arteries. Boulevards.

At seven years of age I invent my first professional aspiration: I will be a road namer, I announce. Hidden away in the bureaucratic labyrinths of city hall, I will staff a cubicle of an office cluttered with dog-eared papers and a jet-black typewriter. My work will entail visiting new lanes and highways, applying my talent for seeing their essence, and giving them appropriate titles. Horse Street, Pine, Down-the-Mountain — these are some of my earliest choices.

The idea for the job comes to me in Florida. The family is here basking in the success of our ancestor's efforts in the Seminole Wars, 1836–1843. It is here that General Fightin' Joe Hooker has tested his youthful mettle on the desperate natives, already runaways from a 1704 rampage, and his efforts have cleared the land and legal system once and for all for the United States citizens of the future.

We are those citizens. Our vacation getaway stands high on toothpick stilts beachside of Estero Boulevard, a once-sandy Indian trail now tarred to facilitate a projected stampede of sunbathers and sports fishermen from the North. My vision of the place, researched over thirty years of two-week stints of sunbathing and tarpon fishing, is the story of a sleepy shrimping village mutating, via stampede, into superhighway high-rise condo-infested urban sprawl.

President Thomas Jefferson gives Meriwether Lewis and William Clark explicit instructions. They are to locate "the most direct and practicable water communication across this continent for the purpose of commerce." They are to "fix" geographic positions by astronomical science. They are to research "the habits, locations, and vocabularies of the native inhabitants" and study the "soil and face of the country."[1] The instructions are suited not just for the fur trade we are told the explorers will accomplish. They are suited for wholesale imperialism.[2]

Lewis, Clark, thirty-six woodsmen, an Indian interpreter, and Clark's African slave York. It is May of 1804, and the group rows a huge and heavy keelboat from Saint Louis up the Missouri River to Fort Mandan. Caved-in banks and shifting sandbars line the course, and rotting buffalo carcasses bob through the waves. The men paddle to Three Forks. It is now June. They are sweating buckets as they haul their boat up slopes, through rock gullies, around stands of prickly pear. Braving rain, hail, and snow, they cross the Bitterroot Range of the Rockies. At Yellowstone, the troop encounters the great grizzly bear the native people have warned them about. At first, using rifles, they shoot the bears flat. But the animals come on bigger, taller, stronger — until downing one requires a dozen shots to the head and chest. At Clearwater, the men burn snag-logs to make canoes and ride the rapids down the Snake River to the Columbia. They follow its enormous bends all the way out to the Pacific Ocean.

In a dramatic gesture rivaled only by Neil Armstrong's leap onto the moon 164 years later, William Clark stands in the sleeting rain overlooking the ocean and carves his name into a pine tree:

WILLIAM CLARK

DECEMBER 3RD 1805.

BY LAND FROM THE U. STATES

IN 1804 AND 1805.

Not thirty years later, after a stint on the road-building project from D.C. to New Orleans, Captain Benjamin Bonneville embarks to the Rocky Mountain wilderness. He is armed with instructions from the War Department. Make special note of British settlements. Investigate "the quality of the soil, the productions, the minerals, the natural history, the climate, the Geography and Topography, as well as the Geology of various parts of the Country within the limits of the Territories belonging to the United States, between our frontier, and the Pacific." Study the Indians, the instructions dictate, "most import, their manner of making wars and a state of peace, their Arms, and the effect of them, whether they act on foot or on horse back, detailing the discipline, and maneuvers of the war parties, the power of their horses, size and general description; in short, every information which you may conceive would be *useful to the Government.*"[3]

(Snowflake Martinez isn't one to ride on the trail. He sees things, ways the land snakes and dips, ways it remembers, and he follows these.

Just now he is reining his sorrel off the edge of the trail, past a boulder adorned with petroglyphs of circles and arrows. In the arroyo beyond, we find a sand wall, tall as an old cottonwood, carved into the terrain by centuries of water streaming from the mountains down toward the Río Grande. Snowflake guides the animal, his hand angling from side to side above the saddle horn, and stops so close to the wall he blends into its face. My pinto and I edge to it like an echo.

The air is shaded and cool.

"¿Che?" Snowflake is pondering something. "¿Che, from where do your people come?"

"Now *that's* a question. Most Anglos wouldn't know how to answer."

"¿No?" His forehead wrinkles like the side of a rock. "¿Por qué?"

"We get displaced, we move, memory is lost. . . . I can *try* to answer."

"Por favor." He stands straight up in the saddle and then settles back down into a comfortable posture for listening.

"I met this woman from the Okanagan band in British Columbia. It was 1991, the year before 1992, you know, five hundred years, when Columbus came. She inspired me to find out who my people are."

"¿How did she do this?"

"She told me she could never be a real friend if she didn't know who I am. Then to show me what she meant, she told me who she is.

She said that her mother was a River Indian. Her great-grandfather was a salmon chief and caretaker of the northern part of their ancestral terrain. Her father's people, she said, were Mountain People, hunters; their medicine came from the spirit of the hunt. Then she said that she was telling me what her place in the world is, what her responsibility for that place is. . . . I decided right then and there that I would mark 1992 by researching my people's story on this continent. I felt I owed this to myself because all people before these times have known themselves by ancestry and place. And I owed it to the natives whose lives were disrupted by the arrival of my people. I owed it to them not to forget."

The sun is slowly ferrying its way into our haven below the sand wall.

"¿Y qué, what did you find out?"

"My people on my mother's side came here in 1633. They were English and French and German and Dutch. My father's side I know less. They were Irish and Scottish and Welsh. Before that, they were all of the Celtic and Germanic tribes of northern Europe, hunting and fishing people like those of my Okanagan friend."

"When your people got here," Snowflake offers, "los indios of my people were already here. The others, we were just coming at the same time."

"It's amazing to think about."

"Sí . . . los antepasados, they were just like us."

The sunlight is now streaming onto our horses' rumps.

"My earliest ancestor on this continent was a minister named Thomas Hooker. He had a big fight with the leaders of the Massachusetts Bay Colony. He wanted more rights for the people. And so he and a band of followers went south on horseback and with wagons. There were no roads then, you see. Just Indian footpaths. They got to a place, not too far from a bay, with lots of oaks and maples. My ancestor was the founder of what became Connecticut. In his biography it says that he 'preached on Sundays and fought Indians the rest of the week.' He and his group launched the first Indian war in North America. They killed a thousand Pequot and took five hundred more as slaves."

"¡*Jees*, Che!"

"Yeah. Jees. . . . I hold this inside. It's part of who I am. . . . My people were hurt, and they went on to hurt others." Just then I notice a desert mouse. She appears tentatively on a ledge in the rock, sniffs our rather substantive presence, and darts into her sandy hole. "After a while, the people in Connecticut sent some of the families west. They expanded their territory to a place they called the Western Reserve. Again they went in wagons, again on Indian paths. My great-great-grandparents, my great-grandparents, Mimere and Pipere, my parents — all were born in Ohio. My brother lives in Ohio now. I was one of the first to leave, to follow a trail west. First to California. Then to these mountains."

"¿Y qué es tu responsabilidad?"

"What it is, well, you see . . . ah . . . it's lost. Because of how we are removed from the land. Because of how food is made in factories. Because of cars and airplanes. Cities. Television. Everything that's happening to your people right now, how the common lands are being taken away and your culture shattered and blown away, it all happened to mine a long time ago. Only slower. Over a longer period of time. From within. . . . I've seen old photographs of my family in Ohio with their big vegetable gardens. Pipere on horseback. I can reach back and find fragments of my people's connection to the land. My uncle drowned in a canoe." The sun is coming around now to alight on our horses' manes. "My family are hunting and fishing people. More recently we are doctors and ministers, inventors and political activists. My grandfather on my father's side was a healer, a homeopathic doctor. I'm not living in my ancestral place. I'm not even sure where that would be. But my responsibility has to do with healing. Knowing spirit. Finding the way. Setting out . . ."

"¿Como traveling these horse paths?"

"Yes. Only this time traveling them in the footsteps of the folks who made them.")

The road lays the way. When you take it time and time again, or even for the first time, there is a feeling of permanence to the route. It is there. It seems as if it had always been there. Not even the touted presence of old settlers' cabins or an Indian village is enough to convince you otherwise. Columbus Avenue. Army Street. Sutter. Kearny. Kit Carson Way.

In the city of my childhood, Millionaires' Row is that strip of Euclid Avenue stretching between 21st Street and 40th Street. I am familiar with this district not because our family ever approached the standard of wealth required, during its late-century heyday, to reside there, but because my mother and I pass through its 1950s shell on our way to a downtown appointment. And because of memory. My mother tells me about the families (I come to know their names), the mansions (which belonged to whom), the stories (madcap adventures). During my mother's childhood, the industrialists and bankers drew into their "society" the lawyers, doctors, and smaller merchants who served them, not as peers exactly, but perhaps more accurately as accomplices. My mother's voice is hoarse as she speaks at once with excitement and distance, with humor and awe — but most of all, with the fascination schoolgirls bring to knowing the details of celebrities' lives.

Millionaires' Row: the very soul of the intersection of empire with industrialism. It is a wide street with a tree lawn generous enough to hold a tennis court, laced with majestic oaks and maples and buckeye. Each home reflects the quirks of its owner. The Herman Frasch residence is a gabled mansion with mahogany woodwork, exquisite stained-glass windows, and a dining hall that seats fifty. Leonard Hanna's estate is made of yellow brick, trimmed in white marble, and sports four two-story pillars across the front porch. Samuel Andrews builds the largest home in Cleveland: one hundred rooms of Victorian elaboration, complete with stone-castle turrets. And in 1876, J.D. Rockefeller himself makes his permanent residence in a stone house on the corner of Euclid and 40th.

The Euclid Avenue of 1880 appears on maps as the authoritative artery running from Public Square at the west (where the industrialists locate their offices in tall buildings named for themselves) eastward toward the apple trees and farmhouses of the Ohio countryside. The twenty blocks dubbed Millionaires' Row have been selected because their situs offers an unobstructed view of Lake Erie, whose shipping lines are given a nightly clink of crystal and ice for their complicity in amassing the fortunes that build these mansions on Euclid Avenue.

The progress of industrialization creates the streets; the streets are built to progress industrialization. Unfolding here is a story that resides beyond mere cause and effect. This is a story of unfathomable ellipsis. "I know an old lady who swallowed a fly," sings grand Aunt May as she bobs me on her knee.

I don't know why she swallowed a fly
Maybe she'll die

I know an old lady who swallowed a spider
That riggled and jiggled and tickled inside her
She swallowed the spider to catch the fly
I don't know why she swallowed the fly
Maybe she'll die

I know an old lady who swallowed a bird
How absurd to swallow a bird!
She swallowed the bird to catch the spider
That riggled and jiggled and tickled inside her
She swallowed the spider to catch the fly
I don't know why she swallowed the fly
Maybe she'll die. . . .[4]

In the beginning, the millionaires travel up and down the boulevard in horse-drawn carriages. The first horse-drawn streetcar appears in 1883, the East Cleveland Railway extending its line from East 55th to Doan Brook, then to East 177th at Euclid. The Payne Avenue line opens. Superior Avenue extends to East 79th. The routes crisscross the city as pathways of manure, laying the pungent lines of economic necessity in thousands of people's lives.

No streetcars are allowed along the section of Euclid Avenue designated Millionaires' Row. Such an infusion of horse droppings, clattering carriages, and people from God-knows-where would be a vulgar and tasteless intrusion into the elegant neighborhood.

Accomplishing this small coup of privilege does not require a full-blown grassroots political movement. It requires nothing more than a raised eyebrow, a tilt of a head, a sigh over Scotch-on-the-rocks — for the very layout of the city's streets is conceived and executed by the menfolk who inhabit Millionaires' Row.

They give the new streets names. Not Horse Street or Pine or Down-the-Mountain but names inspired by the heroes and qualities they so earnestly admire. Euclid Avenue is named for the Greek geometer. In a world constantly expanding in all directions, indeed mathematics neutralizes the fright of dislocation. Euclid is criss-crossed by a grid of streets: First, Second, Third. There is Carnegie for entrepreneur Andrew Carnegie, Perry for Admiral Oliver Hazard Perry, Sterling, Bond, Bank, Superior.

Starting in 1890, bicycles fill the streets. The Rockefellers and Wades and Hannas eagerly purchase the new machines from a host of entrepreneurs who recognize an economic opportunity when they balance it between their thighs — Winton, Stearns, Gunning, Crescent and Sherman — all of Cleveland. Academies for teaching the art of cycling sprout like fine dancing schools, as does a whole fashion of riding habit featuring knickerbocker trousers and argyle socks.

But the true signature of Millionaires' Row is the automobile. The first car is purchased by Dudley B. Wick in 1899. This splendid vehicle is a Locomobile Steamer built by the Locomobile Company of Westboro, Massachusetts. It looks like a beefed-up bicycle, constructed as it is by two welded bike frames onto which is mounted a wooden Stanhope body, with a fourteen-inch boiler seated beneath the driver's chair. It costs $600. Wick's Locomobile sees in its wake a virtual eruption of excitement between 21st and 40th Streets. Soon there are Oldsmobiles and White Steamers and Model T Fords. Mayor Tom Johnson, who resides in the ivy-covered mansion at 24th, purchases a two-cylinder Winton. The rumble seat is invented. And Cleveland itself — with its thoroughfares of cobblestone, mud, and asphalt, with its horse paths and trolley tracks — becomes an automotive manufacturing town.

In 1907 Mr. Walter White surprises everyone: he drives his White Steamer as far away as Wilkes-Barre, Pennsylvania.

(The trail across the badlands has been pounded into the dust by Snowflake's father and his grandfather before him. Eventually, the path makes its way from the desert floor up into the foothills to merge with the hunting trails, lined by piñon and ponderosa, that weave through the mountains.

We come to a road. The encounter is startling after knowing only the freedom of the wind. The road appears unnatural with its over-lay of tar and harsh-yellow lines. A man, an American, is standing blonde and angular next to an aluminum tripod mounting a survey-or's glass. The horses twitch at the sight of him in his orange vest, and the metal clop of horseshoe on hard surface causes my pinto to jump nervously to one side. We are alert now, Snowflake and I.

We see that the road plunges south down a hill from this place of encounter. Roadworkers hauling plastic bags, all of them Chicano and Indian, trudge along the thoroughfare picking up discarded beer cans and dirty diapers. A tiny dot of a vehicle whizzes by them, mounts the hill with no hint of effort, and growing larger by the sec-ond, rushes toward us. The car is a late-model Lexus. As it passes, I catch sight of the license plate: OHIO.

"I hate roads," murmurs Snowflake. "They get your mentality all tied up."

The surveyor jerks his head up to look at us. "Where did you come from?" This is the very question we have been discussing. But before accepting our response, he barks his own answer. "That land is BLM. Should be fences around it."

Before the Americans arrived in full force to these parts, there was just a wagon track used to cart chile peppers and firewood, mutton and manzanas, from one village to another. And there was an unmappable web of footpaths and horse trails. The present highway has been built within Snowflake's memory in a titanic effort involv-ing dynamite and earthmoving machines and hordes of road crews, most of them local men made poor by the confiscation of their land after colonization, being paid now to construct the very venues of invasion that will further destroy their way of life.

"Are you changing the road?" I ask the surveyor.

"Yeah. We're widening it. Yeah, and there's the new four-lane cutover that will go through that sorry patch of dirt you just rode out of."

Stiffening, Snowflake spurs his horse forward across the tar and into the sorry patch of dirt on the other side. I follow. We ride along in silence for a time that is marked only by the creak of saddles and the wind dancing the tears off our cheeks. Finally, Snowflake speaks, almost in a whisper.

"They tried to move the road from one side of the river to the other."

"I didn't know. How strange."

"Sí, y the villages got together y went to the hearings they had."

"You spoke?"

"I was mad, pero I spoke. I learned something. I learned they pretend to listen. Y then they do whatever they want anymore.")

Lincoln Highway — the emblem of American empire. Conceived by Carl Fisher, the highway represents an Olympian salute to the European fiat to expansion. Shortly after Labor Day in 1912, Fisher throws a dinner party for automakers at the Old Deutsche Haus in Indianapolis. When the plates are cleared and the coffee served, the man who just the year before has paved the Indianapolis Speedway in brick bares his dream. *"A road across the United States!"* He is shouting. He is breathless. "Let's build it before we're too old to use it!"

Manifest Destiny is a breathless endeavor. I am feeling breathless as I contemplate it: pony expressing, canal boating, turnpiking, steamboating, locomoting, ballooning, flying. In 1861 the first electric words are shot across the continent via telegraph. After the Civil War wrenches north from south, east-west stagecoach service tries awkwardly to tie the continent back together. In 1869 the golden spike is hammered in, and the Union Pacific provides velvet-upholstered transport coast to coast. New towns sprout. New roads.

1914: eighty-five percent of the Earth is controlled by empire. The production of motor vehicles exceeds the production of wagons and carriages.[5] The Lincoln Highway becomes the means to solidify

the recently closed frontier into a single entity. It will boost business
opportunities across the land, push the known envelope of capital-
ization (Howard Johnson, Ford Motor, Gulf Oil), facilitate military
defense for the nation.

> The Lincoln Highway! Yes folks, it's the Main Street of
> America. Trucks and jalopies and limousines, they all follow
> Highway 30 over the Alleghenies to Chicago, and through
> the fields of corn and wheat to the Rockies and the Sierras,
> and on west to the Pacific. Yes, this is the road that links the
> farms, the mines and mills of America. . . .[6]

"New York! New Jersey! Pennsylvania!" chant American school-
children. "Ohio! Indiana! Illinois! Iowa! Nebraska! Wyoming! Utah!
Nevada! California!"

The highway begins in the most important center in the most
important city, Times Square, on a paved street called the Great
White Way. After a ferry ride across the Hudson River, it picks up an
old footpath widened after 1665 to accommodate wagon wheels.
Then, following the resultant King's Highway toward Philadelphia,
it retraces Lancaster Pike, the eastern gateway to the West.

Freedom. Rochester. Forest. Delphos. Fort Wayne. Chicago
marks the end of eastern civility, the true beginning of the Wild
West. Joliet. Mooseheart. Mechanicsville. Honey Creek. Beginning
in Omaha, the highway is laid over Lewis and Clark's Oregon Trail.
Silver Creek. Odessa. North Platte. Ogallala. Lodge Pole. Parades,
bonfires, songs and speeches, auto shows, fireworks, and flag-wav-
ing catapult an entrepreneur's breathless vision into the new
American craze.

Truckee. Emigrant Gap. Dutch Flat. Gold Run. Road guides
appear in 1901, at first describing the way not by bird's-eye view but
by lived experience: the appearance of a boulder in the road, which
stand of oaks provides shade, the color of the barn where the road
veers to the left. The Jones Live-Map Meter comes next. Precise
road instructions are printed on a disk that is turned by clock gears
connected to the wheels. As the car moves forward, the disk turns
and commands appear: "TURN RIGHT!" "AVOID MUDHOLE!"

Altamont. Hayward. Oakland. San Francisco. Gulf Oil invents the free gas-station road map in 1913. Rand McNally publishes its first *Road Atlas* in 1924. Columbus Avenue. Army Street. Sutter. Kearny.

The land is slicked with petroleum tar. Modern-day settlers embark, carrying their worldly possessions strapped to the rumble seat. More bushes and trees than you can count are flattened dead. White-tailed deer, turkey, and mountain lion flee for their lives. The diversity of the plant world is lost as weeds colonize the highway's edge. Fisheries are clogged with oil from crankcases and oil-change stations. Walking paths disappear. Horses are outlawed. Landslides proliferate. Armed patrol cars multiply. Heavy metals — lead, zinc, cadmium, nickel — are spread freely into the air.

The takeover of the North American continent is under way.

The Lincoln Highway begets more highways. Let's build them before we're too old to use them! Automakers, trucking companies, asphalt and oil corporations, steel manufacturers, road contractors, engineers, rubber entrepreneurs, governors, mayors — all lobby to build more roads. If the 52 million cars in the United States were actually *on* existing highways at the same moment, quips Senator Case in 1955, each would have only seven hundred feet to drive.[7] President Dwight Eisenhower and Senator Albert Gore push through the 1956 Interstate Highway Act to authorize the most massive road-building project in history: 44,000 miles of megahighway.

Road builders press knee to oak plank and pray. "O Almighty God, who has given us this earth and has appointed men to have domination over it," they implore, "who has commended us to make straight the highways, to lift up the valleys and to make the mountains low, we ask thy blessing upon these men who do just that."[8]

For every $1 million spent on the $27 billion system, these men use 16,800 barrles of cement; 694 tons of coal; 485 tons of pipe; 76,000 tons of sand, gravel, and crushed stone; 24,000 pounds of explosives; 121,000 gallons of petroleum products; 99,000 board feet of lumber; 600 tons of steel; 57 brand-new bulldozers.[9]

The takeover of the North American continent is complete.

THE HOUSE

Its belly is always full of good things.

— Frantz Fanon, *The Wretched of the Earth*

Few maps bother to show the location of the settlers' houses. Land-use maps do. Developed by the Land Utilisation Survey of Great Britain, these maps lay a scheme that has since become convention. In it, houses are colored red.

I have in my possession a relic that reveals something of my family's location on the land-use map of imperialism. It is a British magazine article written in 1899, "The Queen's Private Apartments at Windsor Castle."[1] The queen we are discussing is the grand Victoria, who reigned through the final thrust of British dominion from 1837 to 1901 and, with her elegant taste and formal carriage, provided the very definition of an era.

As I peruse the photographs of Windsor Castle's drawing rooms in all their gold-gilded splendor, I am struck by an odd twist: the style of my great-grandmother Harriet's home on Cleveland's East 89th Street is laid bare before my eyes. I have never seen the interior of this house, for its heyday lasted from the late nineteenth century up to the 1940s. By the time I am born, the house has passed to another family, yet I do recall my mother pointing it out on one of our drives downtown. And here I am now, holding a dog-eared leather album containing photographs of the very house.

I presume these pictures were taken in the early 1940s. The driveway is boasting a 1937 Dodge sedan, and family law dictated that no one maintain an automobile for more than five years. Plus, the window shades are blackout opaque, an artifact born of the fear of German air attack during World War II.

I have always thought of the 89th Street house as midwestern, although it did strike me as dark and gloomy in a Victorian sort of way. Now, with these Windsor Castle photographs in hand, I see that the house represents a blatantly earnest striving toward a template of style, class, and functionality — a template fixed in the European mind and expressive of a grandeur only truly available to the recipients of the spoils of empire. The difference between the two sets of memories is not success; both are successful. It is scale. Queen Victoria is the recipient of the grandest spoils of the grandest empire. Were she to stroll into great-grandmother Harriet's house, it would be immediately apparent that Her Majesty was both at home and at the same time engaging in some grotesque act of slumming. Her Majesty's Grand Corridor, after all, occupies two sides of the castle's quadrangle, displays the most magnificent blossoms from her own conservatories at Frogmore, is lined with a 440-foot crimson carpet woven especially for her. Harriet's is, in the end, just a house.

Look here. In the queen's corridor stands a collection of white marble busts. The pièce de résistance is a recumbent sculpture of Her Royal Highness Princess Elizabeth of Clarence, daughter of William IV. The corridor's ceiling is cream-colored and gold. The draperies are of the richest crimson silk damask. And yet "handsome as the Corridor is in itself," pronounces our nineteenth-century magazine writer, "its chief claim to notice arises from the beauty of its *contents*":[2] gilt candelabras, oak cabinets and gold boxes, antique china — Chelsea, Battersea, Dresden, all represented by their most elegant pieces. On every wall hang priceless canvases, huge portraits and nature scenes painted in oil by the most renowned European artists, set in heavy gold-leaf frames.

Now here. In Harriet's sitting room, on the mantle, rests a white marble bust of the god Apollo, whose inspirational contributions to the Greek Empire are well documented. Everywhere, on every table and every shelf, sit exquisite "contents": freshly polished candelabras, china plates from the American colonial period, ivory elephants brought back from a colleague's African safari, a plethora of framed photographs and bronze statues of Scottish terriers, the preferred canine companion of the royal family. A soap statue of a naked woman sits in a glass cabinet as the prized expression of the family humor. The butt of a "standing" joke, the statue is originally carved in an upright posture, but as the August heat has its way, the woman melts into the very recumbent position of Princess Elizabeth of Clarence. On the walls there are immense oil paintings of family members and historic characters framed in gold leaf. Why, over the mantle in the dining room hangs an imposing portrait of French Emperor Napoleon Bonaparte himself.

And here. Take a look at this shot of Harriet's sitting room. On the cherry end table rest a fat porcelain teapot, painted with golden birds and bamboo stalks, and four squat teacups. In fact, the Chinese influence is everywhere evident in the room. The floor sports an almost wall-to-wall Oriental rug, and I can spot six Chinese vases. At least three of the oil paintings on the wall display clipper ships gliding across the sea.

The clipper is an American invention. The British capture one during the War of 1812 and reproduce it for the task at hand: to transport opium through the treacherous northwest monsoon from India to China. You see, the British East India Company in Bengal, the very one that muscles out the local weavers, has a nineteenth-century–style bright idea. The clipper, capable of beating into the formidable China Sea like no other ship, carries the opium England forces Indian farmers to grow. The Chinese buy the drug. *England makes money* — and buys Chinese tea, silks, and porcelain to sell in Europe. *England makes money* — and sells British textiles and machinery back to India. *England makes money* — and becomes the lord of the most profitable triangle of "free trade" in the history of merchantry. In 1770 a mere 15 tons of opium are carried from India to China. By 1900, with the aid of the deft clipper, Chinese addicts are smoking 39,000 tons.[3]

Back home in Cleveland, who can detect that such underhanded activity is going on? Certainly not Harriet or great-grandfather Frank. Anglophiles to the bone, they lounge naively in the sitting room and entertain beneath the striped awning on the veranda, sipping their Earl Grey, their Gunpowder, their English Breakfast on Blue Willow china.

Coincidentally (or not), the explosion of global trade in stimulants like tea, coffee, and coca mirrors the demands of the industrial revolution on the human organism. As urban bustle, factory work, and mechanical clocks come to regulate life's rhythms, the English consumption of Chinese tea skyrockets. "It's four o'clock. It's *tea*time!" they enunciate from the drawing room. In 1669 the British East India Company ships a measly two canisters of tea home to England. By 1900, imports are 400 million pounds. Use of sugar, brought over from the colonies of the Caribbean, jumps from twenty pounds per person in 1850 to eighty pounds by 1900. And as the industrial revolution surges forward, the English worker no longer breakfasts on locally grown grains and native herb teas. He gulps down Argentine beef sausage, eggs shipped from China, and a cup of imported tea sweetened with sugar from the tropics.[4] In the United States, tea goes out with the Boston Tea Party. But the urge to down stimulants in the face of a sped-up, mechanized lifestyle only grows, eventually finding its satisfaction in America's own imperialist ventures. "Hey, buddy, can you spare a dime for a cup of coffee?" After 1865, United States exploits expand to Central America, where local gardens and communal farms are twisted into "free-trade" coffee plantations. Coffee consumption shoots from five pounds per person to 13. Sugar use jumps from 18 pounds to 79.[5]

Properly fortified for their modern lifestyle, Harriet and Frank feel only ennobled by the military "adventures" that bring these new foods to the table. Look here. Lying like sheaves of onionskin on the desk is a stack of letters that Frank wrote in the 1880s. Before he settles in with Harriet at the 89th Street house, Frank serves in the United States Navy as a cadet midshipman on a journey to the Orient. His letters home are collected into a book called *Letters from the Asiatic Station, 1881–1883.*

As well he might be, great-grandfather is concerned about injustice. "It is one of the most *unfair* things I ever knew of,"[6] he wails. Oddly, he is not talking about the horrors perpetrated by the imperial effort; he is aghast at the inequality of conveniences between the midshipmen traveling on the man-of-war and those on the mail steamer. He goes on to reveal his view of native people. "There were no white people at Pago Pago," he observes, "nor were there any stores. This race of people were justly described by someone as the 'Lost Tribe of Israel' from their resemblance to the Jews in one respect, that of getting everything out of you and giving you nothing in return."[7]

("¿Quieres comer, do you want to eat?" Snowflake asks. "I bring a lunch for you."

My back feels like a slab of plywood as I dismount. We lead the horses down a trail forged by coyotes to a wondrous green breath of shade below, and we tie them to the thin trunk of a juniper. Snowflake unfastens a Mexican serape and two old Levi jackets, rolled up like bedrolls behind the saddles, and lays them on the ground. Then he lifts a woven bundle out of his saddlebag. I plop my brittle body onto the jackets and await his gift.

Snowflake's eyes are set deep into his forehead, so deep his straight black lashes are enveloped by skin. With meticulous care he unties the bundle and shows me first two flour tortillas stuffed with beans, green chile, and turkey, then a glass bottle filled with apple juice. His eyes are sparkling in anticipation. "This place, these trees, this shade — es como una casa, a house, ¿qué no?"

"Snowflake, where did you get this food!?" I take a mindful bite out of the burrito. A peppery tang infuses my consciousness like a troupe of flamenco dancers marking fiesta.

"I have turkeys. Ramón y yo, we are sitting around the house a few days ago, y Ramón says, '¿You think it is about time we kill the turkey?' And I say, 'Sí, about time.'"

"How do you kill a turkey?"

"I get it by the neck, ¿qué no? Y I sit on it so it doesn't flap the wings. Then I cut its throat. It only takes a minute for the bird to bleed. Then I pluck it. To roast a turkey, you have to leave the skin on. If you're not going to roast it, you can just skin it. The feathers and everything come out with the skin."

"¿Y los frijoles?"

"Sí, bueno. I grew them down by the river behind my mother's house. In Spanish they're called delabolitas, little round white beans. I don't know if they're the black-eyed peas you call them in English or not."

Snowflake's horse shakes herself free of the juniper. My pinto lets out an urgent neighing sound, almost like a scream of alarm, and Snowflake gets up to investigate. He slowly edges over to the escaping animal, coaxing her with promises he may or may not keep. She does not resist, and he grabs the reins and leads her to the tree.

"I didn't grow the wheat for the tortillas," he says as he sits back down. "My dad, he used to grow wheat over there where we had the orchard. We used to fill up wagonloads of wheat, a big old flatbed full, y we would go up the monte where Malaquías was blessed to have a threshing machine. You could also use goats to walk on the wheat."

He throws his head back in reverie. I sit motionless trying to imagine.

"I'm a mediocre tortillero," he muses. "I make them, you know, y I like my tortillas. Pero I go to mi tía's house. She has made tortillas her whole life, y there's nothing better. All I know is some people make better tortillas than other people. I like them soft."

"These are soft."

"Sí. Mi tía made them."

My insides are chuckling with delight — at the music of Snowflake's voice, at the caress of cool air rising from the grasses around us, at the peppers lingering in mouth and mind from this homegrown burrito.

"The chile is from Domingo Archuleta's field. I worked on his old Bronco, the one he uses to go hunting, y he traded me this chile. I peeled it y roasted it myself. . . . For a while they brought in that Number 9 Chile. People used to plant it over here, pero we didn't like it. 'Number 9' they call it, I guess because it grows nine inches. It was a real big chile with lots of meat, pero it was never as tasty as the one from here. Ours is little y wrinkly. It doesn't have so much meat, pero it's got a better taste."

He pauses for a moment, as if asking his taste buds to guide his thoughts. "¿You know the apples they sell nowadays, those big old

Washington apples? They're real nice on the outside, ¿qué no? all dark y pretty. The other day I bought apples at the store. ¡Aaaaa-iiii! Take a few of these, the sign says to me, y I did. ¡Híjole, I got cheated! You could have painted a picture out of them, pero they tasted like sawdust. . . . Now this juice here . . .ʺ

"It tastes like heaven."

"Sí, sí, el cielo. Mi abuela's trees.")

Grandmother Mimere is born to Harriet and Frank in 1890. When Mimere is eight years old and the Spanish-American War just beginning, the *Washington Post* prints an editorial purporting to sum up the mood of the country. "The taste of Empire is in the mouth of the people," it pronounces, "even as the taste of blood in the jungle."[8] Spain cedes Puerto Rico, Guam, and the Philippines to the United States. Cuba gains independence. Mimere *lives* the heyday of classical imperialism, and yet in her lifetime, she also witnesses its demise. After World War II, the principal imperial structures fall apart: the British, French, Belgian, and Dutch empires disintegrate between 1945 and the early 1960s. Britain alone loses dominion in Australia, New Zealand, Hong Kong, New Guinea, Ceylon, Malaysia, the Asian subcontinent, the Middle East, East Africa from Egypt to South Africa, Guiana, the Caribbean, Ireland, and Canada. Still, the profound link between my grandmother's life and the British Empire is evidenced by the fact that she refers to her mother as "Victorian." She describes herself with the more modern term *Edwardian*.

I do not need photographs of Mimere's house on Stillman Road to stir memory. I am born just after World War II and spend the happiest days of my childhood poking through the crannies of her domicile, delighting myself with the fairy costumes that so whimsically echo our European pagan heritage, playing double solitaire with Mimere and her Make-Checks-Payable-to-Clara deck of cards.

How deeply and yet subtly we inhale and exhale the breath of the empire: imperialism is in the air! Queen Elizabeth's coronation in 1952 is so historic an event that the family trundles over to Mimere's to stay the night, awakening at some ungodly hour to witness the pomp and circumstance on Mimere's brand-new black-and-white television. I am taught, always, to view the cultural contents surrounding my life as normal: the British Empire is, after all, normal. "The earth was made for Dombey and Son to trade in, and the sun and moon were made to give them light," announces the first edition of *Dealings with the Firm of Dombey and Son* that grandfather Pipere holds in his collection of original Charles Dickens memorabilia. "Rivers and seas were formed to float their ships; rainbows gave them promise of fair weather; winds blew for or against their enterprises; stars and planets circled in their orbits, to preserve inviolate a system of which they were the centre."[9] Now as I make these mental wanderings among Queen Victoria's Grand Corridor, Harriet's sitting rooms, and Mimere's library, I am struck again with the undeniable echo of the British Empire occurring in, of all places, Cleveland.

A foray to the bell cabinet is a requirement of every visit to Mimere's house. Four shelves house a voluminous collection of handbells: hundreds of bells, bells from Japan shaped like the Buddha, glass bells, china bells, bells with horseheads for handles, bells that look like English thatched-roof houses. My favorite is a brass bell in the shape of a lady-in-waiting. The handle is her torso, the bell jar her skirt, and the clappers hang down as shapely little legs replete with stockings and Mary Jane pumps.

Mimere uses a handbell to ring for the maid, and Irene appears in her white dress and apron. When the familiar tinkle breaks the stiff air between courses, Irene hastens out carrying the next platter, perhaps a Yorkshire pudding or ice-cream molds in the shape of miniature Christmas trees. At holidays she is joined by extra "help" — usually an African-American woman whose name we never learn. When the tinkle shoots out from the master bedroom, Irene scurries up the servants' staircase to deliver a soft-boiled egg and pot of Earl Grey tea.

During my childhood, I am delighted by the bell cabinet. But I never grasp it in its true role as museum to the essential imperial dynamic, the master-servant relationship. This I realize only today as I read about the queen's private apartments at Windsor. "Her Majesty's writing-chair, with cushioned back and footstool below, stands in front of the writing-table," writes our author. "At the right stands a Japanese shelved table bearing stationery cases, letter baskets, etc.; another table near by holds the latest published reference books, bound in Royal Red morocco and gold. Yet another table contains the small gold handbell which calls *Her Majesty's attendants*"[10]

(After our sumptuous meal and a moment of midafternoon shut-eye, Snowflake and I mount the horses. My back feels more relaxed.

"¿You know something?" Snowflake is talking softly, almost as if conversing with himself. "We used to walk everywhere. Or else we would catch the Vigil's burros. When a car went by, mi abuelo used to say, 'There goes an American,' because the only people who had cars back then were the Americans. ¿Sabes?"

He switches now from reverie and begins to talk directly to me. "I like you," he says. "Pero I grew up not liking the Americans.")

I do not know until just now why I have harbored a fascination with that class of Britishers that, during the changeover from the old landed system of dukes and peers to the incoming economics of colonial capitalism, holds onto its castles but has no resources to keep them up. The peasantry, responding to the economic forces of first the communal land theft that is called enclosure and later industrialism, is wrenched from the land to work the factories in Lancashire and Liverpool. The still-landed inhabit the skeletons of their former distinctions — with no firewood to heat the cavernous rooms, wallpaper peeling off the walls, Oriental rugs discolored by mouse urine.

Due to the shifts in economic accumulation after World War II, the Glendinning family is clearly not of the same social stature and clearly does not have the resources of the previous generation. Yet my mother meticulously raises us with all the order of her own Edwardian childhood and a pinch of the gentility she knew in her Victorian grandmother's world. This effort, while it provides lightness and stability, also passes on a mostly intact template of imperial assumption.

"We have none but Chinese servants on board and they are the best boys I ever saw," great-grandfather Frank has written. "They make splendid boys for waiters, they are excellent cooks, and are exceptionally clean and neat. . . . I am thinking of buying one when I get over to China and bringing him home with me. They only cost ten dollars and would make, together with the monkey, quite an acquisition to the household."[11]

Slavery is falling from favor at the time of this reflection. The Civil War has seen to that, and yet the change does not usher in equalitarian community. The services previously provided by slaves are now accomplished by live-in servants who are paid in lodging, board, and small amounts of cash. After World War II, a trend away from the rigid class lines set in place during classical imperialism arises, and the people who perform these same services become "maids" and "help" who live elsewhere and are paid entirely in cash. From what I can gather by listening to the grown-ups, it is becoming increasingly difficult to find "good help" (read: nonrebellious slaves). We have good help; we're not talking lady-in-waiting handbells, but good help nonetheless.

Hilda comes every Tuesday. Like Irene and Helmut, she is from Eastern Europe. She makes me a soft-boiled egg at noon, and she teaches me my first sentence in a foreign language: "Gib mire te," a phrase perfectly calculated for a young girl destined to become the lady of the next generation's house. On Thursday morning at seven-thirty — rain, shine, or ice blizzard — Violet flings open the back door. She is African-American and lives in Cleveland's ghetto Hough area. She fixes me a peanut butter and jelly sandwich.

The two women do not wear white dresses with aprons. They wear whatever they want, and as I grow older, I find myself hanging around with Violet by the warmth of the dryer, listening to her stories. In this minuscule way, the rigid formality of one master-maid relationship shakes loose. Outside the seeming innocence of our friendship — for after all, servants and their masters' children have always maintained the possibility of caring — the enforced rigidity of the imperial dynamic is remarkably breaking down. Decolonialization is succeeding all over the world: India achieves the stunning feat of independence from Britain in 1947; one hundred formerly colonized peoples follow suit.

Algeria. Guiana. Cambodia. Vietnam. Laos. Iran. Malaysia. Burma. Ceylon. Palestine. Nigeria. Cuba. The civil rights movement is under way as well. In 1955 Rosa Parks refuses to sit down in the back of an Alabama bus. By 1961, blacks and whites are traveling together through the South in the infamous Freedom Rides. And the arising postwar economic order will formulate a class system conducted less by the old colonial bloodlines, more by an as yet unidentified nouveau riche of an increasingly transnational yet American-dominated corporate system.

Nonetheless, the Glendinnings have maids. One is a woman of color, the other borderline "white," and through these relationships breathe deep-seated echoes of imperialism. Plus, the house on Edgehill Road is gracious. We have "contents": antique colonial china, a couple of heirloom chairs, some leather-bound books, Paul Revere silver. But no one can get away with comparing the Glendinning home to Windsor Castle. What is missing is the expansiveness produced by the servants' quarters; there is no other house-within-the-house, no other kitchen for the maids to take their meals, no other staircase for passage to answer the bid of the mistress, no other set of bedrooms. My mother is not a grand lady or a matriarch, and she doesn't build her identity on the fashions of British royalty. My mother is a 1950s housewife. She listens to "Bob and Ray" in her pink spoolie-curlers while percolating vacuum-packed Maxwell House. In the living room hangs a long sash of woven wool with a brass ring sewn to the bottom end. If we were alive at an earlier time, my mother laughs, we might pull the sash to call the servants. But since we are alive in midcentury, the sash is "decoration."

An unnamed transition is under way, detectable at first only by the silent passage of old-world artifacts into museum pieces, then as the rising global economy begins inserting itself into our every breath, with new artifacts and new assumptions. Every house on the 2500 block of Edgehill Road sports a new washing machine and a Davy Crockett coonskin cap, and this same "perfect" life with these same "perfect" artifacts is reflected back to us on TV.

But let me tell you the truth: no one knows what is going on. The air surrounding us seems shattered in fragments, hovering, brooding, heavily drifting one way and then another.

I am coughing in the playroom. My lungs, scratchy like the skin of a Brillo pad, explode into cacophonous peals. Hundreds of books set into the built-in bookcase race by, my vision blurred as I heave into the atmosphere. My mother walks in unexpectedly with Violet in tow. She is going out, she announces; Violet will take care of me. An unwelcome tickle lashes up my throat like a lick of fire; I double over in yet another rampage of coughing. "You just did that to *show* her," my mother accuses. "*You*'re not sick!" And she bolts out through the back hall toward her car.

Chrysler Imperial. Windsor. Crown Victoria. Princess. Clipper. Bonneville. You might have known my father. He graduated from Harvard University summa cum laude in 1938. He received a degree in medicine from Western Reserve Medical School.

Then, in 1951, he begins transporting me and my brother in the new Packard out to the sanitarium. He is the president. Part old people's home, part mental institution, the place smells like a mixed drink swirled with bandage adhesive, Mercurochrome, and desiccated skin flakes. Canned minestrone and hot dogs are served at the long table in the basement kitchen, and then Dad shepherds us into the examining room. It is here, on the examining table, that he launches a twelve-year career as an imperialist.

"Git up on the table!" he barks, using a tone ostensibly at odds with the breeding assumed by a Harvard education. And then, with his penis, he wrenches open my brother's tiny anus and relentlessly punctures the delicate flesh. As if treating me for a medical condition, he forces my legs apart, insists I pretend pleasure with penetration. He drags us by hair and legs through the halls, encarcerates us in the mop closet, threatens to give us illness, bloodlettings, operations, death. "I'm giving you my disease!" he thunders. And when I return to my mother, mute and dissociated, migraine flames shrieking out the pain, the "good doctor" overrides the meaning of my affliction, calling it "fear of old people" and "something little children go through." When my mother finally decides to keep me home, he steals from his conjugal bed and, pillows stuffed over my face, rapes me in the house. He takes us on "Sunday drives" in the Packard in the LeSabre in the Cutlass, assaults us in a flower nursery, and draws others into his game — other children to harm, other adults to be our dominators, adults whose names I can still recite. My father finds endless ways to perpetrate what becomes his life's work. And as with the British lord in imperial India, the work gives his life meaning; it is what he breathes for.

I am watching television numbly in the house on Edgehill Road. I am the child of empire — surrounded by Chinese teapots and Oriental rugs, regaled with stories of the exploits of my ancestors, raped by my father, forced to witness the torture of my brother.

Will we survive? I ask, not fully understanding why this is a question I must pose. Who is that angry bald man slamming his shoe against the table? I wonder. Why are there everywhere maps of a place called Suez? Why do the grown-ups talk incessantly about the past as if it were magic, about the present not at all? What is wrong with this ideal and unchangeable moment called America?

THE GARDEN

Death from the city. Wilderness from the city.
Wildness from the city. The Cemetery. The Garden.
The Zoological Garden.

— Susan Griffin, *Woman and Nature*

SMASH THE GARDEN PARTY!

— Graffiti at Jones and Green Streets, San Francisco

The map displays the plan of the garden. It shows hedges and a lawn surrounding the house. A wavy rock path, edged by summer flowers, leads from the front door to the boundary of the property. The garden is a poem.

The map delineates the geometric configurations of the garden. Each section is given shape by a scheme of pathways radiating out from a central fountain. Surrounding it, rectangular areas display ponds adorned with goldfish and waterfowl. The garden is a mathematical arrangement of the natural world.

The map reveals the shape of the concrete cells erected for each specimen: round for elephant, rectangle for lion, square for bear. The garden is a cage.

The map shows the full construction: the three-part access to the cour d'honneur, the grand château encircled by elaborate plantings, the cross-shaped water axis, and the main section replete with parterres and bosquets, topiaries and temples. Do not overlook the

51

open-air theaters and, pleasing to the eye even on paper, the long boulevards stretching into the distance. The garden is a spectacle.

The map shows the natural world in its place within the empire.

Mimere limps along the rock path across the lawn, leaning into her wooden cane for support as she calculates each jerk of a step. She aims for pleasantries against the pain. We have a joke in the family: whenever anything disappears — a pair of scissors, a lick of stamps — it is said to have been swallowed up by the exotic ground cover *Pachysandra terminalis* that surrounds the driveway and yard. "Everything goes in the pachysandra," it is said, and at this moment my grandmother attempts to sway attention from her halting gait by asserting that yet another item — in this case, the ball of her hip — has been lost in the pachysandra.

She nods at the roses blooming in the rectangular beds around us. Ever so painstakingly, we pass by the gardener's ivy-covered shed, built onto the back side of the garage, housing stacks of terra-cotta pots and tools forever caked in dirt. We come to the sundial, set upon a waist-high stone pedestal. Roses are positioned everywhere around us — red roses, yellow roses, white roses — and daisies and alyssum and azalea.

Mimere walks only so far as the sundial because this is where the walkway ends. An arched trellis guides me into the next section of the grounds, a kind of wild transition area whose grass grows scrubbier through the jutting elm roots. I pass through a second archway into the vegetable garden. Here I find straight rows of corn, lettuce, parsley, tomatoes, squash, potatoes, anise. I crouch down to fulfill my mission in the garden: I pull four carrots from the earth and gingerly carry them back to Mimere for our lunch. The garden is our secret world. It is peopled by flowers and stones and trees, and by our friends the fairies, Mrs. Tittlemouse, and Peter Rabbit.

It is said that the term *garden* is at root the word for yard. Gierd, geard, gardin, jardin: enclosure. It is said that the *enclosure* movement virtually wastes local sustainability in the nation-state that boasts the model for Mimere's garden. Beginning in 1770, the English Parliament privatizes 6 million acres of previously commonly held fields, meadows, wetlands, and forests. Other arrangements, illegal, strip a near equal acreage from communal use. The upshot: 97 percent of *all* land in England comes to be owned by individuals and companies poised for the moneymaking promises of industrialism.[1] A way of life instantly dissolves. Traditional cottagers, freeholders, and tenants are forced off the land, are turned into hired hands, become factory wage slaves, deteriorate into welfare recipients and beggars. No more cutting fuel and furze, no more small-scale farming, no more pasturing, no more foraging, fishing, or hunting. "Inclosure," as one man tells author Arthur Young in 1804, "was worse than ten wars."[2]

("Che, your people, they have no land, ¿qué no?" Snowflake's brow is darkened by an urge to understand.

"That's right. No land. Everybody buys their food at the store. Nobody remembers how to hunt or grow."

"¿Sabes cómo resultó esto, do you know how this happened?"

A breeze picks up my hair and blows it helter-skelter across my shoulder. All knowledge of myself flies with it. "No . . . I don't . . . not exactly."

"Che, aquí toda la gente sabe como perdimos la tierra, everybody knows. Mis tíos tell me. Mi padre tells me. Everybody."

"How did it happen?"

"This land here, this river, these trees." Snowflake juts his lips east toward the Sangre de Cristos. It is hard to glimpse the full expanse of land he is pointing to. We sit on our horses below the foothills. But I do see peaks in the distance, raw and granite to the sky. "This land es La Merced de Frijoles. It is ours."

"When you say this, the sign at the road — U.S. FOREST SERVICE — seems thin, like an apparition."

"Somos como fantasmas, we are like ghosts, too. Pero in the beginning, we were indios made from this land. Mi abuela was Tewa from Oke Oweenge, San Juan Pueblo. We were indios from México: Toltec, Azteca, Mayan. Y we were the settlers the Spanish brought here, some of us Spanish, but also Moor, Arab, African, even Irish.

Pero those conquistadores, los shining metal, they just left us here. First they said we were part of New España y then México, y we had las mercedes, el campo común, the land grants. When los norteamericanos came, they agreed, it is written in the Treaty of Guadalupe Hidalgo, las mercedes were ours still for always, it is written, Che."

"What happened?"

"Oh . . . so many things happen."

I turn my horse in a half circle in the sand so I am sitting face-to-face with Snowflake.

"The Americans sent the survey people. Y the first thing is they made the paper say the land is smaller than it is. Then the lawyers came. They told las familias they know how to make the paper right. Pero the people had only sheep y horses, no dinero. So the lawyers said, 'Give us land for what we do for you.' Sí. We did that, we gave the lawyers land. Next comes La Floresta y El Bureau of Land Management. It happened that the Forest Service y BLM put their fences around *our* mercedes. *¡They picked the exact same land!* Then they said, 'You are no good at taking care of the land, you don't know enough, we will help you.' Pretty soon, la tierra has signs up all over y roads that did not exist before. Y they are calling the Frijoles Land Grant 'public land,' ¿qué no? They took care of the land by making us pay to do the things nuestros padres did for nothing. Hunt, fish, get firewood, the sheep. They took care of the land by letting big companies come in y do strip-mine y clear-cut, things we never knew how to do. Y then the land does not look like it was."

I feel a jolt, electric lightning cracking my gut.

"Pero, Che. This is not all before. ¿Do you see? It is a lot of rocky *now*. Last year, mis primos, they had land. They were growing chile y keeping burros como siempre. La Floresta says, 'We are going to survey. We made a mistake.' So they send the survey people, y suddenly the paper says mis primos *owe* La Floresta sixty acres. Y the next day the signs go up. The land is gone. It is La Floresta."

"Their blood must have boiled."

"Sí. Su sangre boiled.")

Empire begins with access to bargain-basement land and materials. It is propelled forward by the destruction of sustainable lifeways and the generation of uprooted people desperate enough to work for wages. The process occurs both within the empire and at its edges: enclosure within, colonization at the edge. Then, in due time, enclosure and colonization meet up with industrialism and "free trade." It is a raucously hopeful meeting: they throw a party.

The garden is the site of the party.

That the garden is artificially arranged is given: *everything* within empire is arranged. How the garden is arranged, though, is ever changing. Giovanni Dellini's *Allegory of Earthly Paradise*, painted not a year before Cristóbal Colón's first voyage, depicts a walled garden paved in geometric tiles with a lone potted tree in the center. Two hundred years later, British theologian Thomas Burnet reasserts that the world would be truly divine were the land flat, the seas arranged in regular shapes, the stars thrown into the sky in geometrical pattern.[3] European gardens of the period surround their estates with geometric parterres and straight-line plantings. Hedges manicured to look like wedding cakes superimpose a predetermined puzzle that, experienced both close-up and from afar, proposes an illusion of human-made order. As the rolling countryside is highjacked for enclosure and the industrial revolution transforms village life into factory sprawl, gardeners revolt from the insistence on geometric nature. Mechanistic work schedules, train departures, pocket watches: too much of life is mathematically determined as it is. The new landscapers soften the lines within the enclosed yard, let sculpted trees grow natural, mix wild with domestic.

We witness here the psychic dynamic that plagues imperial society from its inception. Back and forth, back and forth: control versus freedom, fascism against democracy, order fights nature, kings against natives, ideology challenging experience. In the context of the control required to maintain imperial order, the urge to freedom becomes irrepressible. It erupts; it is crushed. It erupts again; it is crushed again. You may hunch your shoulders in resignation. Such is human nature, you may sigh. And yet in our not-so-distant past,

before the maps and the roads, before the kingdoms and the concentration camps, the urge to freedom is daily asked and daily
answered. Only the iron clench of what social philosopher Lewis
Mumford calls "the Megamachine," meaning imperial order and its
attendant technologies, casts freedom as the losing proposition.

I tug at my grandmother's cashmere sleeve. "Mimere," I sheepishly
croak. I am harboring the thought that our secret garden is a place
where we might share secrets. "Mimere. Daddy hurt us. He took
needles. Daddy rammed his pee-pee in . . ." — I clutch between my
legs — ". . . pussy."

I do not learn this word on "The Howdy Doody Show" or at
Saint Paul's Episcopal Church. It is a word I hear barked from my
perpetrator's throat as he arranges my quivering body into porno-
graphic pose.

The slap from her hand, the sting from the pearls on her bracelet,
they hit like a hatchet to a turkey's neck. "Never use such a word!
NEVER!!" She grabs at my collar, and I jump from her bony reach
and scurry down the garden path.

Versailles. Yes, this would be a good time to tell the story of
Versailles. Truly it is the story of the Battle of the Gardens for, in it,
a subject of the French King Louis XIV is sentenced to life impris-
onment in the fortress at Pignerol for . . . *planting a garden.*

And what a garden it is! Vaux-le-Vicomte is erected on the very
site where three villages once thrived. The financier Nicolas
Fouquet wipes out the villages with the aid of 18,000 hired labor-
ers, many of them villagers themselves. His motivation is not to
realize the sort of garden in which a cultured man might take pleasure with his friends. It is less to provide seclusion. His purpose is to
build a stupendous theater for grand-gala fetes in the grand-gala
French imperial tradition. Fouquet's goal is to stun. In order to
achieve this goal, he hires Le Nôtre, heir to the position of first gardener of the Tuileries, to design a horticultural spectacle visible in a
single glimpse.

A single glimpse is immediately visible — to the king himself. Le Nôtre leaves a grove of trees on either wing of the central chain of parterres, framing a vista, carrying the eye forward, forbidding it to roam to one side or the other. On this set he places fountains, statuaries, and smaller gardens upon which a guest might happen with surprised delight. The folly produced by this construction is not so much in the amount of fertilizer required to maintain the topiaries but in the going conception of absolute monarchy. It is said that Fouquet might have saved himself by doing precisely what Thomas Wolsey, across the channel, did with Hampton Court. "Why on Earth would a subject build himself so magnificent a palace?" is the question. The answer: "To present to his master." But no. Fouquet wants Vaux for himself. He throws two grand-gala fetes to display his spectacle, and the poor king, tormented by accounts of these affairs, arrests Fouquet and throws him, garden gloves and all, into the dungeon.

The king then sets Le Nôtre upon his hunting château at Versailles, ordering him to create not a single star as he has for Fouquet but a veritable constellation — eleven square miles of palaces, gardens, boulevards, temples, and pools whose irrefutable purpose will be to erase all memory of Vaux-le-Vicomte. Needless to say, as any student of French history can tell you, he succeeds. Versailles becomes the most talked about garden in all of Europe.

(The trail east of the paved highway ascends from the pink sand and scraggly juniper of the badlands into the foothills of the Sangre de Cristos. The sun is reaching for its peak, and Snowflake and I are relieved to be heading away from the road toward the rustle of ponderosa needles.

"Se llama this trail Frijoles," he twists back to tell me. His dark eyes are glistening again. "It follows el Río Frijoles to the land grant."

We climb up and up along a thin trail bordered by pines of all sorts. Then we dip over a sandy ridge. Below, in the canyon, lies a paradise of leaves and branches, flowers and grasses, made green and lush by the cascading of last winter's snows. Without words we start the slow descent, horseshoe by horseshoe. Dust flies up from the effort, and there are moments when I clutch the saddle back so I won't topple forward over the pinto's ears.

At the bottom we find the Río Frijoles and a meadow of such verdancy that I let out a squeal. I have never seen so much cota herb in all my life. Cota has been gathered in these parts for centuries, and each summer I pick enough of it to last me the winter. Its concentration of minerals is beneficial for the kidneys, the stomach, for cleansing one's whole system.

"Oh, Snowflake. *Please!*"

"Sí, sí. Podemos pick the yerba."

In moments the two of us have dismounted, tied the horses to branches, and fanned across the meadow cropping the yellow flowers and their long stems. Snowflake strikes up a little song, not unlike a song Winnie-the-Pooh might invent, about medicinal plants.

> *¡Qué bonita!*
> *Cota, cota,*
> *Cardo santo,*
> *Plumajillo,*
> *Dormilón.*
>
> *¡Qué bonita!*
> *Cota, cota,*
> *Cola de caballo,*
> *Culantrillo,*
> *Chicoria.*
>
> *Cota, cota,*
> *¡Qué magnífica!*
> *Flor de Santa Rita,*
> *Dormilón.*

A neon-green hummingbird darts by, and we mosey back to the horses carrying bundles of flowers so generous and wild they barely fit into our arms.

"This is a *whole* winter's store of cota! How will we ever get it home?"

Snowflake rests his bundle on the ground and opens the leather saddlebag flapped over my horse's flank.

"Mira. It will fit. Pa'cá." Some kind of miracle unfolds before my eyes as the two unwieldy clumps are transformed into a luxuriant bouquet cupped in deerhide and framed by the brown and white of pinto hair. "La tierra provides, ¿qué no?"

The sun is hot now, and the flowing water is crooning to the meadow. I grab my daypack, and we walk a few grassy yards to the water and seat ourselves on wet trout-colored rocks. Snowflake breaks off a plumajillo stalk to use as a flyswatter.

"The river sounds like a radio announcer," I observe with urgency. "Do you hear a sound like a radio?"

"I hear only the río." Snowflake casually swats a yellow jacket snooping around his boots and then focuses his whole being on chopping its tiny carcass in two with the stem-end of the stalk. "Pienso que habían farmers here in the old days."

"And they grew beans?"

"Sí." He makes an unsuccessful lunge at a blue fly on my shin.

Searching for a canteen, I rifle through my pack, and to my surprise, a hardback book falls out. Snowflake is quick to catch the book before it tumbles into the water. And quicker still to bring wonder to an artifact that, were it not for my presence, would be inconceivable.

"¿Qué tienes?"

"It's a book I was carrying when I took a friend's daughter for a ride. I forgot to take it into the house."

"¿Qué es?"

"*Winnie-the-Pooh*. Look at the title page. It says, 'To Mary Hooker from Aunt Ellen. December 25, 1926.' The book was a Christmas present to my mother when she was six. She grew up with these stories, and she passed them on to me. I grew up with these stories."

Snowflake mindfully gathers the book into his lap. A hand-drawn map adorns the inside front cover. The map shows the terrain where Christopher Robin, Pooh, Piglet, and the rest of the gang live. "POOH BEARS HOUSE," the map reads. "100 AKER WOOD." "POOH TRAP FOR HEFFALUMPS."

"The story is about a boy named Christopher Robin . . . er, Cristóbal Primavera." We both laugh. Snowflake enjoys it when I mix my English with school-learned Spanish. "Los amigos de Cristóbal were bears y baby pigs y mulas," I joke. "Viven en England."

Snowflake is now leafing through the thick pages with a particular fascination for the line drawings. Here is one of Pooh lying in bed, his slippers perched neatly below the headboard. He is dreaming of an elephant. My mother has obviously taken her Crayolas to the book. The blanket is crudely colored pea-green, the elephant is gray, and the jar of "hunny" encircled in its trunk bright purple.

"¿Qué es un Heff . . . a . . . lump?"

"A Heffalump is an elephant. The word is playful, you see . . ." Before I can explain, Snowflake is onto it.

"¿Como we say *elemento* por *elefante?*"

"Yes. Como así." Snowflake smiles brightly, and the sun-baked wrinkles shooting from his eyes form instant arroyos across his cheeks. He opens to a random page and begins to read aloud.

"But . . . Pooh couldn't . . . sleep," he enunciates haltingly. "The more he . . . he . . . tried to sleep . . . the more he couldn't. He tried . . . Counting Sheep . . . which is sometimes a good . . . way of . . . getting to sleep, and as . . . that was no good, he tried . . . Counting Heffalumps."

Snowflake looks up at me suddenly, locking my eyes to his. "Wait," he urges. "Díme, Che. Cristóbal y sus amigos viven en England, ¿qué no? ¿How can there be elefantes en this story? . . . *No hay elefantes en England.*")

No hay Asian, African, or American flowers en England either. Why, most flowers indigenous to northern Europe bloom only in the spring, and by June all the color is gone. Beginning in the eighteenth and nineteenth centuries, though, summer-blooming flowers arrive. They come in the wooden hulls of clipper ships, in steamers, by iron frigates, carried home by the hand of adventurer, administrator, and botanist alike.

China is a principal contributor for, by happenstance of the glacial period, China comes to boast the richest and most varied collection of temperate flora in the world. The year is 1689, and James

Cunningham slips the seeds of a tallow tree into a makeshift paper envelope and mails them back to England. The Slater brothers, who direct the British East India Company's activities in China, send whole plants via their ship captains. In 1789 Sir Joseph Banks delivers a single specimen of the Chinese monthly rose, and this plant becomes the parent to all such roses in England. Thomas Reeves introduces wisteria at Chiswick in 1818. By 1835, the plant bears 675,000 flowers.

Most important, Reeves directs the work of the Royal Horticultural Society. The society employs Chinese artists to make paintings of plants and flowers, and it hires botanist extraordinaire Robert Fortune. It is claimed that Fortune "exhausts the gardens of China to [England's] gardens' benefit."[4] Anenome. Forsythia. Rhododendron. Honeysuckle. And yet the plants he collects come only from gardens and nurseries in the cities of Macao and Canton. Holly. Cedar. Bleeding heart. Umbrella pine. In 1842 and 1858 new treaties open up foreign botanical collection to as yet unexplored places, including locations in the wild. Charles Maries ascends the Yangtze as far as Ichang, bringing back wild primrose and witch hazel. Augustine Henry exports 158,000 specimens of more than 3,000 species. He discovers that China is homeland to many genera whose origins are previously mistaken or unknown. Lily. Flowering peach. Plum. Apricot. Cherry. Pear. The specimens are transplanted in synchronicity with the urge to plant "natural" — the burgeoning landscape movement — and the English garden is born. Maple. Orange. Loquat. Walnut. Raspberry.

Next, E. H. Wilson treks through the hinterland. He delivers 65,000 live specimens, 16,000 dried plants, and 1,500 seeds. He introduces 1,000 new species for cultivation, including 300 separate species of fern, 60 of rhododendron. Chrysanthemum. Azalea. Aster.

It turns out that the premier British botanist of the Victorian age is my ancestor. Joseph Dalton Hooker, like his father before him, directs the foremost plant-collection center in all of Europe, the Kew Gardens of London. It is he who invents the concept of weeds: "the tramps of our flora," brought in from elsewhere, that usurp the local genera as "colonizers."[5] It is he who reveals the mind-set of ecological imperialism. "We have the apparent anomaly, that

Australia is better suited to some English plants than England is,"
he proclaims in some kind of twisted challenge to the natural world,
"and that some English plants are better suited to Australia than
these Australian plants were which have given way before English
intruders."[6]

Lions. Heffalumps. Cougar. Bear. I come to know wild animals in
the gardens behind my father's sanitarium. The experience is neither
heroic nor playful. Is the good doctor about to rape his children
again? Terror fills the summer air. An island of shrubs and trees
stands in the center ground, but I cannot muster the courage to go
close to it. "Lions!" I sob to my brother. "Watch out! There are
LIONS in there!!"

My mother knows nothing of these lions or any that may reside
within the walls of the hospital. Or in the backseat of the Cutlass. Or
in the flower nursery where my father rapes us. She tells me about
other lions, lions whose four-hundred-pound bodies are memoralized
in the basement of the Cleveland Clinic. These are lions that have had
the misfortune of passing into the sights of Dr. George Crile's rifle in
Britain's Tanganyika Territory — and have since been stuffed and
placed on display in the Cleveland Clinic's wild animal museum. We
have a connection to these lions because our family has done business
with the Criles. The miniature herd of ivory elephants on Mimere's
desk is a gift from Dr. Crile himself.

It is a compelling idea for research, this notion of comparing the
brains and sympathetic nervous systems of African animals with those
of humans. Do peculiarly human diseases spring not from biology per
se, Crile wonders, but from civilization's demands on the human
organism? Yet the mind that thinks up this project is ensconced in the
trappings of the imperial mind. "*At some very basic level . . .*" What else
might provoke one to purchase a ticket from Imperial Airways and trot
halfway around the planet to dissect foreign fauna? ". . . *that is distant.*"
Why else might one so meticulously destroy the natural world for intel-
lectual curiosity? And without offering even so much as a prayer of
thanks? ". . . *that is lived on and owned by others.*" Could divesting oneself of civilized ways (read: empire) be the more scientific approach?

("Alazán, elk is what I know," Snowflake tells me. Just then his sorrel lets out a vibrant neigh, as if remembering all the hunts she has known. "Sí, alazán."

"One time," he begins, "not so far from here, there were alazanes. All night long they were bugling. Mi amigo Oso y I got up at daybreak. We prayed for meat for the winter. Then Oso walked into the forest by himself. I heard a shot. '¡He got un alazán!' I thought. Pero no, he had shot a bear, a black bear. We were so excited that we put it up on one of the mares whole, just slapped it on top. Y here I was leading a mare with a big old bear on top, falling off all over the place."

"Really? My God . . ."

"It was a pain. It just kept sliding off. I told Oso I can't take this bear down this way, so we stopped to cut it up y put it into sacks. There we were in a clearing, skinning the bear. Pero we made one mistake: *we didn't tie the mare.* Before, when the bear was on the mare's back, ¿recuerdas? nothing, *nothing* happened. So we didn't tie her. The mare was just standing there. I was tying the sacks of meat on her. We were almost done. All of a sudden she opens up y full-force kicks both her back legs pa'trás. ¡BONG! ¡BONG! I almost fainted. ¡Aaaaaaaaa-iiiii! I fell to the ground. My head swelled. I couldn't move. Then she went over to where Oso was at, all the time bucking y trying to knock off the sacks, y she kicked him right in the butt."

I am speechless.

"Then it started raining. We came down all injured, ¿qué no?"

I am shaking my head in disbelief.

"Pero we brought back a bear.")

OTHER PLACES

*Only when we are ready to accept risk as part of the
price of having wild bears will we contain the irra-
tional fears and thoughtless habitat destruction that
result in the loss of bears from the world.*

— Paul Shepard, *The Sacred Paw*

The Countess loves any*thing in a pith helmet.*

— Woody Allen, *The Purple Rose of Cairo*

At the start of the European endeavor, the map delineates sharp
boundaries between "us" (motherland, superior, white) and
"them" (foreign, lesser, dark). Using straight lines, distinct patches of color, and elaborate etchings of lions, the map charts the
necessary distance between imperial and native, between what is
ever expanding into other places and what remains sustainably in
place.

In time, though, as empires extend to encompass the globe, the
map attempts something new. It crushes the native's otherness in
a carnal fit of mastication and then colors it, as a European chef
might color the frosting on a wedding cake, the same hue as the
empire itself. England's pastry, from India to the Falkland Islands,
is frosted pink. That which has been swallowed up is made, by dint
of color coordination, as manageable as a girl's matching sweater
and knee socks.

Violet is other. She trudges to the bus stop in her plastic house slippers, coughing up sputum, to travel to a place called Hough, which is dark with tenement buildings and industrial soot. My mother raises her eyebrows. The satin gowns we don at our lawn parties might one day be donated to women in the ghetto: we might see our dresses — she is sweating now — *streetwalking* down Euclid Avenue.

Sweating, indeed. The challenge is poised starkly before us: grasp how other people feel, why they struggle, what they care for and give their lives to. And yet, how can we? Sadly, our hearts come ill-equipped for the task. Our maps and highways, our houses and gardens, they are located in other people's places and are filled with other people's things. We have no idea where we are. Or who.

Names. Names we use to speak of them. Nigger. Wop. Slant-eye. My father spouts these words at the dinner table. Look. The cat is ever so skillfully edging toward the bowl of ice cream when Dad jerks like a machine, pounding his fist on the placemat, and snarls: "Redskin! Mexican! Jap!" The cat leaps into the air and runs.

I balance my brand-new roughout boots against a rock shaped like a calf's head and squint across the unbroken South Dakota landscape. The year is 1963. My brother has stood up to our father in an act so stark and death-defying it has been twelve years in the making: using threats he himself has invented, he forces our perpetrator to stop the abuse once and for all. Truth be told, I cannot grasp that the terror has ended. In fact, my psyche will not believe it until, twenty-five years later, the memories surface from the lock of repression and I begin to heal. For now, I flee the site of relentless brutality by joining an Episcopal mission to Indian country, a modern-day errand to a place colonized during Mimere's childhood.

Against the opaque midwestern sky, I open the pages of my first selection on the required reading list, *Heart of Darkness*. Listlessly, with no interest at all, I begin to read: "The Nellie, a cruising yawl, swung to her anchor without a flutter of the sails, and was at rest. The flood was made, the wind was nearly calm, and being bound down the river, the only thing for it was to come to and wait for the turn of the tide."[1]

Randy places his hand on my shoulder and gently turns me around to face him. He is quick in body, teen Lakota in love with rock 'n roll, and right now he is making a visit to the mission from his home in Fort Yates. We become friends.

"What are you reading?" he asks.

"Uuug," I groan. "It's a book I have to read for school. We have to finish three required books and then two others we choose from the list. It's a drag."

The prospect strikes Randy as more than a drag. It's an outrage, and his mercurical shape mirrors his agitation.

"What?! You have to read books from *a list*?! This is preposterous! It's wrong!"

"Yeah," I whine. "But we have to."

"What did you tell me your school motto is? We learn for life? Can't you see? Life can't be learned from *lists*."

Names. Other names. Not mammy or nigger or wop. But honky and gringo and paleface. Names whispered from the farthest echoes of Mimere's handbell. Names spoken around the world. Wasicu. Bilagáana. Gente de razones. Ahatai. Names used to describe the colonizer. Saltu. Mericano. Qallunaat. Gavacho.

Could there be a more obvious gavacho than Cristóbal Colón? What remarkable absence of sight and care emanates from his personage? What shattering of sentiment lays the basis for his being? Surely it is not a shattering unique to him. Colón is a man of time and place: he is by history and birth a man of maps, an explorer, an imperialist.

Here come the three ships: *Nina, Pinta, Santa María*. Here they come across some 280 days of gray waters, trade-wind clouds, and fickle climes. The tropical old-growth forests of the islands they come upon are unimaginably spectacular. Yet all that we read in

Colón's journal about the land he has so eagerly sought is . . . well .
. . not much that first day . . . and then only such vapid descriptions
as "very large"[2] and "very green."[3] After a month our captain finally begins to notice the flora and fauna. He proclaims "oaks" and
"arbutus,"[4] which in retrospect we know do not and did not grow in
the Caribbean. The "geese"[5] he witnesses are ducks, the skulls of
"cows"[6] most probably manatees, and he calls precious tobacco
"weeds."[7] Our founder is a man lost at the edge of his own map and,
except for a voracious interest in what might translate into commercial wealth, utterly lacking in humility and radically resistant to personal impact. Colón's confessed goal is "to bypass no island without
taking possession."[8] It is to leave in his wake "always . . . a cross
standing."[9]

Let us not even dwell on the despairing condition of the homeland where crosses are standing: the mass murder of its own earth-
based practitioners, the ecological devastation fostered by a view of
the natural world as "desolation" in need of geometric reorganiza-
tion, the filth, the epidemics, the crush of spiritual buoyancy that
leads to overcompensation in enlightenment strategies. No. Let us
zero in on what Cristóbal Colón actually thinks and does when he
meets his fellow humans of this foreign land. "They all go around as
naked as their mothers bore them," he writes in his journal,

> They are well built, with very handsome bodies and very
> good faces; their hair [is] coarse, almost like the silk of a
> horse's tail, and short. They wear their hair over their eye-
> brows, except for a little in the back that they wear long and
> never cut. Some of them paint themselves black (and they
> are the color of the Canary Islanders, neither black nor
> white), and some paint themselves white, and some red, and
> some the eyes only, and some of them only the nose.[10]

It has never been doubted that the people who greet Colón and
his crew are friendly. It can even be said that they are happy. "They
are the best people in the world," Colón remarks. "They are without
knowledge of what is evil; nor do they murder or steal. . . . They have
the sweetest talk in the world, and are gentle and always laughing."[11]

On the first day the natives lavish gifts of herbs and parrots and cotton on the travelers. When the *Santa María* crashes into a coral reef, the neighboring kaseke-leader sends all the people of the town to offload the sinking ship, generously provides the Europeans with housing, and weeps for their loss.

The first recorded sexual act between newcomer and native signals the end of the appropriate use of the word *encounter*. As far as we can tell, it is not Colón who enacts the event. This first account is from the nobleman Michele de Cuneo. "While I was in the boat I captured a very beautiful Carib woman, whom the said Lord Admiral gave to me," he discloses,

> and with whom, having taken her into my cabin, she being naked according to their custom, I conceived desire to take pleasure. I wanted to put my desire into execution but she did not want it and treated me with her fingernails in such a manner that I wished I had never begun. But seeing that (to tell you the end of it all), I took a rope and thrashed her well, for which she raised such unheard of screams that you would not have believed your ears. Finally we came to an agreement in such manner that I can tell you that she seemed to have been brought up in a school of harlots.[12]

Such sensation of specialness attends the penetration to foreign lands! You can see it on the map. This is no hokey pile of sticks and cowrie shells on the beach. There is authority here: threadlike lines of mathematics etched onto parchment, cities pinpointed with splendid calligraphy, mountains painted in purple, oceans boasting tall ships with elegant canvas sails, and in the upper corner, the obligatory royal red and gold-leaf emblem of the monarchy.

Clutching his cartographic scroll in his glove, the imperialist is propelled to project his thoughts onto the people and places he visits. And indeed he does, he does.

The land of the other is ours, he posits. Wait. He is not convinced. The place seems so strange, so remote, so incomprehensible. . . . The other is evil. He slams his fist on the table! No. I am wrong.

She carries herself like royalty, she is gentle, she is happy. . . . The other is stupid and ignorant. But wait. The other speaks to the stars and the wind and knows everything there is to know of the universe. . . . The imperialist is angry now. The other will tumble to deserved extinction! No. The other will be the one, like a cockroach, to prevail. Or perhaps just maybe, through spiritual fortitude, the other will be the one to triumph above us all.

The list is muddled, as confused and contradictory as the mind of the imperialist. It is a list made partially of one's worst suspicions about oneself, now twisted and aimed toward someone else. And in no small portion, it is a list of one's own blocked aspirations and deepest wishes.

But the true center of attention is not the other at all. *It is oneself.* "Rivers and seas were formed to float *their* ships," after all. "Rainbows gave *them* promise of fair weather; winds blew for or against *their* enterprises; stars and planets circled in *their* orbits, to preserve inviolate a system in which *they* were the centre." The true center is the imperialist's own pith helmet. It is his collection of China porcelain, the fineness of his wool jodhpurs. The unyielding focus is the strength of his thigh muscle as he pulls himself up the ledges of the Burundi to the first tender tricklings of the Nile. It is the shake of harness bells on Millionaires' Row. The breathless arrival: Wyoming! Utah! Nevada! California! Cristóbal Colón, Meriwether Lewis — him, no one else, always *him.* The other becomes merely that which resides, like weeds and Africa and the dark of the moon, outside himself — until at last, in his lunge for universality, he swallows it up and colors it pink. Or red, white, and blue.

(Snowflake gives his reins a shake and wonders inwardly, in a Spanish whisper, if we are on the right track. He makes a silent calculation and then spurs his horse up a deer trail to the rise above the canyon wall. Surveying the terrain in all directions, he nods and then calls down to me.

"OK, Che. Ven pa'cá."

I follow somewhat awkwardly, my fingers outstretched all the way up the hill as ponderosa branches conspire to slap me in the face. At the rise I can see our position. Down and to the west stretch sandy foothills, their curves and hollows dotted with juniper in patterns like a dalmation's hide. In the deepest cup of the valley lies our village, appearing from this distance ideal and sweet, a lived version of Robert Louis Stevenson's Land of Counterpane with its tiny pickup trucks bouncing along corduroy roads and little mud houses in place by the river. To the south, north, and east, the mountains unfold into infinity like carpets of green majesty. Everywhere and into the distance there are trees and streams and animals and birds and then, farthest from the valley, raw granite peaks.

"Esta tierra," he curves his arms into a circle as if to gather in the terrain, "La Merced de Frijoles, it is ours. Except La Floresta has their signs up everywhere, y they like to tell us how not to use it. Pero we know it is ours. Over there, pa'yá . . ." He points south where mesas and canyons roll out in front of us. "This is ours too. It's another seven thousand acres. The government gave us our claim in 1891. The Sacred Word says that the south boundary is 'the heights' above el río. La Floresta is telling us the boundary is just el río. Pero we are going to get the heights back."

Snowflake tightens his thighs to urge his horse forward, and we progress over the rise. After a quarter of a mile, he jerks to a stop and points across a cluster of short mounds to a cabin hidden in the hillside. The cabin is surrounded by waist-high stands of mullein and waiting horses. It seems to me another place, radiant with intent.)

When I use the word *capture*, I do not mean the colonial capture of natives. (To be sure, on his second voyage, Cristóbal Colón corrals no fewer than sixteen hundred.)[13] No. I am talking capture the other way around: capture of people from the empire. Throughout the history of European and American penetration into other people's places, there have always been prisoners of war. Sometimes they are solidly complicit with the imperial effort: cartographers, soldiers, blatant attackers. Other times they are merely naive, some would say innocent. Whichever, in capture they are called to witness the agony that imperialism produces — and perhaps experience some of their own.

"The Indians came forth bedizened in their traps and feathers, their tomahawks and scalping knives in their uplifted hands, great daubs of red paint above and below their eyes." Texas Ranger Nelson Lee is captured by a band of Comanches for slaughtering their chief. "They circle round and round us in a spasmodic trot, uttering their hoarse guttural songs." Indeed, it is a harrowing time for Nelson Lee. "Very often, one of them, deserting his place, would dart towards us with his drawn hatchet, threatening to brain us, while another would seize us by the hair and go through the pantomime of scalping."[14]

Adoptions happen as well, occasionally leading to epiphanies regarding ways of living more suitable to human happiness than those previously known. The Irish immigrant Mary Jemison is taken in a raid on the Pennsylvania frontier when she is thirteen years old. After a frightening trip away from civilization and into the forest, the young girl is awarded a pair of moccasins and ritually adopted into the Seneca tribe by two sisters. She is, in her own words, "ever considered and treated as a real sister, the same as though I had been born of their mother."[15] Jemison is content among her adoptive people, enjoying a life moving with the seasons from river to valley, growing corn and squash, and hunting in the wilds. She marries twice and gives birth to seven children. "No people," she reports, "can live more happy than the Indians did in times of peace."[16]

I myself move from river to valley in my life within the empire, prisoner to the seemingly unceasing imposition of trauma and grief. The rapes and torture sessions go on and on. My psyche dissociates at each escalation of assault and with each change in means and method. Then one day, one bright and unusual day, I am invited to cross the boundaries delineated on the map.

Randy and I sit on the concrete step to the bunkhouse. The sky rises above us like a cathedral of blue infinity. The air bulges hot and thick against our skin. We long to plunge into the Missouri River, just ten miles up the road, but the pickup is on its dusty way to Mobridge to fetch soft drinks for the Coke machine.

"Are you ready?" he teases. He takes a folded handkerchief from his jeans pocket and carefully spreads it open on the step. A used razor blade is revealed. I am ready, and I will never be ready.

We have each chosen a source of blood on our bodies so that we may transfuse ourselves into a river that flows beyond the empire that is shaping our lives. My choice is a vein pushing against the skin of my left middle finger, below the second knuckle. Randy chooses a blue line on his index finger. He goes first. I do not watch. When he is finished, he hands me the razor, and I catch my breath to raze the surface of the skin in a single motion. There is blood. We make some comments, now forgotten, about the solemnity of the moment. Then we press our lifeblood together to become blood brother/blood sister.

In celebration, Randy's mother sews me a quilt with red and green diamond-shaped patches, and Randy takes the Greyhound to Cleveland to live with my family. I do not remember the time well. There are photographs of him in the backyard awkwardly attempting, against all odds, to join our early '60s suburban mania. My father, newly frustrated from his orgy of sadism, names Randy "the dirty Injun" and one inevitable night takes him aside in the library, by the encyclopedia of great books, and snarls at him to "git out." Randy attempts to warn me: there is a *real* heart of darkness in the house, he whispers. And then he flees to a boardinghouse on the West Side. Not long after, a letter from the draft board arrives. Randy is captured by the United States military. He sends me a Christmas card from Vietnam. "I'm in a different world over here," he writes. "Nothing really matters but my own will to live. . . . Life and time have stopped. Never again will I take all the simple things like a McDonald's hamburger for granted."[17]

A few days later, right after Christmas, Randy is killed by an exploding grenade near Da Nang.

The empire pays no attention. Its mind is occupied elsewhere; its mind is busy slipping through the other's world, alighting on its exotic shelters and folksy artifacts, emerging replete with metaphors and museum pieces to replenish itself.

Well, OK . . . *replenish* is the wrong word. The acquisitions do not actually satisfy. Perhaps *shore up* is better. Torn apart by the contradictions and conflicts of its own making, empire is in a sorry predicament. And no matter which way you turn, the sorry state persists. The act of imperialism gives rise to a wound that did not previously exist, and every drop of blood gushing from that wound — terror, hatred, despair, worthlessness, revenge — answers not to empire-size inventions of unity and healing. It answers only to the remedy of the original thrust.

Other places, other people. We are drawn to them, we are terrified of them. We dress them in our fashions, we dress ourselves in theirs. Whether they reside at the center of our minds or at the edge, they fuel the manufacture of how things work for us, of what we think and how we feel. Why else the hollow men? This lunge to Africa and Asia, to South America and Antarctica: it is a nervous disintegration. In the privacy of our own homes, we breathe with great expectations, we reside on the beach. We are pride and prejudice, around the world in eighty days, psycho; they, always, the last of the Mohicans.

I am terrified. I want to flee, to travel — the Hough, South Dakota, Vietnam — to return with lion carcasses and rosebushes and Blue Willow tea sets. By the warmth of the dryer, Violet is my ally. By the time she has padded to the bus stop, she has become foreign and I afraid of her.

("This is the place where we are meeting," says Snowflake, whispering as if we have entered a space governed by its own laws. I am stiff from the ride but more alert than ever. To communicate across the interstices created by imperialism, I must be attentive to Snowflake's every word, his every move. I must call upon every shred of history and psychology I have ever learned. At the same time, I must forget it all. Now, through some completely unknown verdict he himself has determined, he summons me to this cabin in the mountains. I have been passing through his world on horseback. Now I truly enter it.

One last canyon lies between us and the cabin. The horses take the lead, traversing the steep hillside in mindful zigzags. My horse's hoof clinks against a rock, and it tumbles in slow motion down to the grassy floor of the canyon. There is no wind here. Our saddles chirp in chorus as if to announce our coming. The other horses catch our song. A plaintive neigh arises from their gathering. Snowflake clicks his spur to his sorrel's flank, and she lunges up the hill. My horse eagerly follows. We are greeted on the slope by curious brown eyes and stomps in the dirt. We dismount and tie our reins to pine branches. Snowflake sits down on a mica-flaked boulder. I join him. He raises one finger to his lips to indicate we must be very, very quiet.)

IN WHICH THE MAP IS ALTERED

Maps have three basic attributes: scale, projection, and symbolization. Each element is a source of distortion.

— Mark Monmonier, *How to Lie with Maps*

FROM DOMINION-PINK
TO TOYOTA-BLUE

MAPMAKERS, PLEASE STAND BY FOR REVISIONS.

— Isuzu advertisement, 1998

Something is going down, and it's not just the strange appearance of heffalumps in England. It's not merely caffeine addiction within the empire or the dark questions of a child. These are by-products, symptoms. Truly, something *is* going down.

And yet the map covers it up, informing us that things are working well. Why, more and more the globe is colored by the hues of imperial nations. Pink. Mustard-yellow. Green. The world is a virtual rainbow. Why, technology is making things better. Clipper ships and then steamships and railroads and airplanes are making faraway places accessible to the reach of civilization. Submarine cables and telephones are providing means for more efficient colonial management. Rapid-fire rifles, submachine guns spouting pistol-caliber ammunition, and then atom bombs facilitate control.

The demise of local self-sufficiency is the crown of it all. Everywhere native peoples are forced off their lands, outtaxed, disallowed their sustainable ways, forced into dependence on wage-serfdom in whatever industry their colonizers choose for them. Forget the armies, bureaucrats, and missionaries that have buttressed imperialism in the past: global hegemony by sheer economic close-out lies within reach.

Misplaced elephants, substance addictions, and children's pain may be our everyday tracking devices. But it is other things, things revealing systemic instability, that catalyze the deadly concern in high places that shapes the second half of the twentieth century. Recession. Depression. Two global wars. The emergence of America as number one. Nuclear weapons. The umbrage of a competing imperialist system. The eruption of decolonization movements.

Instability is a messy proposition for the straight-line columns of bank accounts. If a global system of capitalist control is to succeed against the specter of communism — or more dangerous, against the specter of local self-sufficiency — a more stable form must be lined up.

Look at the map.

1940 Mexico. The people, mostly natives and mestizos living on ancestral lands, grow all the corn, beans, oranges, sheep, and medicine they need to live. Mexico is a patchwork of land-based communities.

(A mountain village east of Española, New Mexico: Snowflake Martinez is born to a family of once-Mexican farmers and sheepherders. It is a painful birth. His mother cries out loud, and blood is splattered on the mud walls of the candlelit room. The Martinez family is jubilant.)

1944 It is summer-hot in New Hampshire. An occasional maple leaf drops onto the windshields of the mirror-black Packard and Dodge sedans that pull up to the Mount Washington Hotel in Bretton Woods. Corporate executives, financiers, bankers, and government leaders disembark in a mood of dark concern. They are sensing instability. In between slabs of roast beef, ice-cream molds in the shape of American flags, and demitasses of Colombian-grown coffee, they situate the United States at the center of a new, improved capitalist world. The U.S. dollar, they decide, is to be the standard by which all other money is measured. They envision the World Bank and the International Monetary Fund to facilitate their efforts to expand corporate capitalism around the world.

("Los norteamericanos took our land, y we got to be poor," Snowflake whispers. "Then Los Alamos Lab came. Al fin everybody had to work for American dollars.")

The way it was is not the way it is;
the way it is becomes how it will be.

1945 The United States displays its newfound dominance, blasting three atomic bombs across the global brain.

A U.S. warship bobs prominently on the waters of the Suez Canal. King Ahb El-Aziz Ibn Saud of Saudi Arabia boards with great decorum. President Franklin Roosevelt receives him and, over tea, promises military protection in exchange for American access to oil.

1946 Television is launched.

The map of corporate vision extends magically plastically in black and white (in Technicolor) north south east west to encompass the globe.

1947 Dominion-pink recedes. India wins independence. Pakistan follows.

I am born in Cleveland, Ohio. It is a Demerol-scapolomine-
ether birth in a sanitary green-tiled room. In celebration,
Mimere picks up the lady-in-waiting handbell and rings for
tea service.

American Telephone and Telegraph scientists invent the transistor, paving the way for the miniaturization of electronic circuitry.

1949 President Harry S. Truman makes an anthropolitical proclamation. Self-sustaining peoples are "underdeveloped," he pronounces. The industrial nations of the North are "developed," the chosen, the front-runners, he announces. All others are stragglers lagging behind in the race whose finish will determine the definitive expression of human accomplishment.

The World Bank and the International Monetary Fund open their teller windows, offering economic growth of the front-runner brand.

They extend money to underdeveloped and newly decolonized governments so that they — potential bargain-basement providers, producers, and consumers that they are — can build global-ready industries. Mexico borrows. Chile borrows. India borrows. Everybody borrows, innocently entering, not the definitive race as they are told, but a nasty snare that will immobilize them for generations to come. Now they *owe*.

The Soviet Union officially enters the race in the front-runner division, blasting its first atomic bomb.

1950 Indonesia breaks from Dutch rule.

> *At Mimere's house on Stillman Road, a family portrait is taken. The grown-ups sit in the center of the picture but seem on edge. They nervously speak of their rose gardens and of World War II. No one mentions what is happening now.*

1951 A young father in Cleveland takes his children for a Saturday drive in a Packard sedan. He pirates them into the basement of a hospital, then tortures and rapes them.

> *I think you may know my father. Harvard University, summa cum laude. He is sticking needles into my brother's penis. He is using tweezers to yank out the baby teeth that stand in the way of ramming summa cum into our mouths.*

1952 Americans spend $16 billion on television sets.[1]

1953 Tokyo. A struggling research company housed in a shack purchases an AT&T license to manufacture transistors. The company is called Sony.

Enter the biologists. The intimate geography of the cell becomes known: the landscape of genetic inheritance is discovered in DNA.

1954 The landscape of communism is rejected. Senator Joseph McCarthy searches under every bed for subversive-Commie-pinkos: heads roll; mothers and fathers are jailed; *The Selected Works of Thomas Jefferson* is banned. The race tolerates no questions.

Vietnam breaks from France.

1956 Morocco, Egypt, and Sudan achieve independence.

(Snowflake goes on his first hunt. He and Jaime Sandoval ride their ponies through yellow-leafed forests into the land grant territory of their fathers. The two boys shoot a deer, cut it up with hunting knives, carry it in sacks back to the village.)

1957 Africa's Gold Coast overthrows Britain to become Ghana.

Sputnik sails through the cosmos, opening infinity to a race of orbiting eyes and ears.

1959 Cuba achieves independence.

1960-1 Nigeria goes free. Senegal too — and Madagscar, Republic of Congo, Tanganyika, and South Africa.

In a Deep South town, where the atmosphere of slavery lingers like humidity on the skin, African-Americans are assembling, marching, protesting. During one mass arrest the police chief questions a nine-year-old, "What's your name?"

The boy gazes straight into the chief's eyes and answers: "Freedom."

1962 Algeria breaks from France; Uganda, Trinidad, and Jamaica from England.

Packing nuclear, United States President John Kennedy and Soviet Premier Nikita Khrushchev face off over Cuba.

> *The insides of our guts are quivering all-out terror. God is dead! The world is ending! Nothingness reigns! As if to salve our dread, Revco Discount Drug arrives. Its warehouse approach to cosmetic sales is situated on the new commercial strip by the racetrack on land that just last year was farm. We girls lay our allowances on the counter in exchange for pale pink lipstick. My father threatens to kill me if I tell. He buys me a transistor radio. I jam it to my ear, drawing out every note of "Louie, Louie" from its tinny little delivery as I lounge across the four-poster bed where he rapes me on Saturday night.*

1964 North Vietnam. President Lyndon B. Johnson launches all-out war. Farmers are murdered, soldiers gassed, women raped, the lush countryside turned into bombed-out moonscape. The goal: to corral this headstrong people, kicking and screaming in their jungle camouflage, into the corporate economy.

> *At risk of bloody retaliation, perhaps death, my brother stands up.*
> *"I will tell!" he trembles to our father in a fit of crazed courage.*
> *"I will call* THE POLICE!*" Twelve years of torture ends.*

1965 Indonesia. It does not end everywhere. U.S.–backed troops slip into the newly decolonized rice paddies, murdering a million of the country's craftspeople, small-shop owners, and farmers in what seems at once revenge for preferring sustainability and a strategy for eliminating land-based culture.

(As a poor rural Chicano, Snowflake Martinez is a prime target for induction into the U.S. Army. He runs.)

> *I run from my father and his tea-stained world.*

1968 U.S.A. Millions flood the streets to protest the Vietnam War.

> *I dodge the flying wedge of the Oakland Police. I am bombed*
> *by CS gas dropped from a helicopter on the Berkeley campus.*
> *During a mass march down Shattuck Avenue, I am hauled*
> *away in a frosted-window bus and jailed at Santa Rita*
> *Detention Center.*

1969 In one of the all-time public relations moves, the National Aeronautics and Space Administration engineers something *spectacular* for us: it rockets a steel-girded capsule of men to the moon. One of them jumps and leaps and waves a stiff American flag.

> *We watch cynically in a commune on Vine Street.*

(Snowflake watches cynically in the general store of the village.)

The map expands to the limits of the technological imagination: mustard moonscape now — Jupiter Mars the black infinity of space.

1971 Sony expands its operations beyond national borders, opening the first Japanese electronics plant on United States soil.

Intel Corporation designs the 4004 microprocessor, a circuit made of thousands of transistors on the tiniest fleck of silicon.

Shit happens: I become ill and I don't know why.

1972 Stateless money happens. The far-flung effects of the expanding economy catalyzed at Bretton Woods fly in the face of the nation-state as a self-contained bank account. Good-bye gold standard! The fixed American dollar gives way to ever-fluctuating, ever-transient capital on paper. Banks and corporations now have the capability to move money to and from their worldwide operations with a phone call, to extend markets to any place under the sun, to hold sovereign governments hostage by threatening to pack up and take their jobs with them: in essence, *to use land and people anywhere any way they want.*

Landsat I is the first remote-sensing satellite to provide a spectral-band portrait of the whole Earth.

1972 The tragedy of Bretton Woods-style domination is revealed. Corralled into a race of someone else's making and handicapped in their run, "underdeveloped" and newly-decolonized nations cannot pay back their loans. The World Bank imposes austerity programs: slashing wages; eliminating aid to the displaced, unemployed, and starving; devaluing local currency; flinging open the borders to hypernational investment; eliminating all opposition.

Chile. Thousands of ordinary citizens are tortured.

My father buys me a Sony tape recorder.

1973 Biologists discover that a dividing cell injected with genes from another cell reproduces endless copies of the foreign genetic material.

A once self-sustaining country is injected with foreign capital.

1974 Diner's Club invents the credit card.

How it is.

1975 North Vietnam defeats the United States.

How it will be. Three million Vietnamese have died. The United States has massacred not just the people but the land, dropping more explosives than were used in all of World War II. Farms become toxic swamps, forests smoking craters. "National independence simply leads to take-over by a new brand of colonialists," reflects historian Erich Jacoby. The Vietnamese must now forge survival not as the self-sufficient people they have shown themselves to be — but against the dictates of global capitalism.

The tragedy of decolonization is revealed. Given the insidious contamination of their societies by empire, new ruling elites reproduce, in Pakistani Eqbal Ahmen's words, "a new pathology of power."[2]

Dictatorships emerge. Fundamentalism. Inter-ethnic violence. Civil war. Trauma. Suffering.

Muzak fills our heads.

1979 Drugs fill our veins. The Central Intelligence Agency allies with rebel opium armies in Afghanistan against Soviet forces. Heroin from the Afghani mountains pours into the United States. Drug-related deaths in New York City rise 77 percent.[3]

(Snowflake's brother, Hipolito, is found cold dead in his trailer behind the drive-in in Española.)

I qualify for MasterCharge.

1980 Corporate ownership of the genetic maps of living organisms is no longer science fiction. The Supreme Court awards patent rights for bacteria to General Electric.

1981 Hewlett-Packard produces the superchip. It can multiply two 32-bit numbers in 1.8 millionths of a second.

Meanwhile, from the plush wool carpet in the Oval Office, President Ronald Reagan hurls curses at the "Evil Empire." All-out terror. We are quivering again.

The urge to freedom is irrepressible. It erupts; it is crushed. It erupts again; it is crushed again.

1982 It erupts. Millions of protesters march to end the nuclear arms race.

Impossibly in debt, Mexico gives in to World Bank austerity. Already maquiladora-factories cluster along the Mexican side of the border — taking advantage of wages one-tenth those in the United States, nonexistent environmental laws, and corporate-friendly tax breaks. Under austerity, regulations are loosened even more. A stampede of foreign investments is unleashed. The number of maquiladoras quadruples. Local businesses fold. Poverty skyrockets.[4] The industrial solvent xylene peppers drinking water at fifty thousand times the level allowed in the United States.[5]

Those CEOs, politicos, and bankers, they are feeling as insecure as ever. They are putting their wallets together again, plotting now to break down every known barrier to their goals. They want access to every last rain forest and gold mine in the world; they want the consumerization of every nation and village on Earth.

1986 The Uruguay round of the General Agreement on Tariffs and Trade begins. Behind closed doors, in some unknown location, the bankers and executives and government leaders discuss things you and I know nothing about. Wherever they are, whatever they decide, slabs of Argentinian beef and Colombian-grown coffee are served on fine china.

1988 In a mass rebuff of communism, the Soviet empire fractures into sovereign states.

The race is on: running hard and fast. Not against anything now. Just for itself.

McDonald's sets up franchises in Moscow.

Desperately in debt, the Mexican government breaks up its traditional cooperative ejido farms and signs all rights to corn production to U.S. corporations.

The inner map of an animal may now be owned, engineered, and sold. Du Pont wins patenting for its "Harvard Mouse," a rodent that, because it is injected with human genes, is predisposed to cancer.

1989 The socialist and communist nations of Eastern Europe fall. Golden arches sprout in Prague and East Berlin. Forty-seven of the top one hundred economies of the world are not nation-states but transnational corporations.[6]

(Snowflake's cousin Rudolfo is jailed for gathering downed firewood on his ancestral land grant.)

1990 Mexico. Seventy-five percent of the people now live in poverty.[7] Forty percent of all beans are imported.[8] Children in the streets of Mexico City beg so they can buy Frito-Lay corn chips.

1991 The U.S. blasts into Iraq with bombs and uranium-tipped bullets in a brief but TV-ready war to prevent Saddam Hussein from expanding into oil fields claimed by American corporations. Afraid that his privileged protection from the U.S. might be in jeopardy, King Fahd invites President Bush to station military forces on Saudi soil.

Systemix, Inc., wins the patent rights to human bone marrow.

How it is. Your skeleton belongs to Systemix.

British-owned Pillsbury moves its Green Giant broccoli and cauliflower operations from California, where workers are paid $9.00 an hour — to Mexico, where they get $4.28 a day.[9] McDonald's feeds 22 million people each day.[10]

> *It is said that 37,000 family-run shops throughout Europe will fold under the financial duress of corporate imperialism, to be replaced by 300 corporate supermarkets.[11] It is said that what workers are left in the developed nations will soon earn salaries equal to those in the undeveloped. It is said that the speed and pervasiveness of corporate supercomputers — from banking to satellite surveillance — make possible the massive exchange of data and money that provides nonstop fuel for the economy.*

If the map could show us the General Agreement on Tariffs and Trade as a product, it would be a rubber stamp. GATT gives legal legitimacy to what has already come to be.

The way it is.

Gucci. Rolex. Oscar de la Renta. Club Med. United. People who buy Toyota trucks jump straight up in the air.

1992 Seventy-five percent of all corporations are based in North America, Western Europe, and Japan.[12]

An American child witnesses 100,000 acts of violence on television by the end of elementary school.[13] Wal-Mart opens a new store every three days.[14] Its yearly revenues top those of Indonsia.[15]

How it is;
How it is.

Peasants in India become criminals for using the twigs and leaves of their sacred neem tree. Half a million farmers and their families, wearing threadbare saris and scarves, march to Bangalore to protest the patenting and corporate ownership of their ancestral plants.

(Snowflake buys a neat little package of sunflower seeds at the supermarket. Beautiful flowers grow — with not *one seed* inside to eat or plant anew. Snowflake does not understand how this could be. If he wants to plant sunflowers again next summer, he will have to *buy more seeds*.)

Free trade: freedom for corporations and banks to go wherever they want — from the moon to the DNA of your bones.

I buy a small house in a village in northern New Mexico.
1994 Mexico. The Zapatista National Liberation Army seizes the main cities of the province of Chiapas — demanding real democracy, land reform to return stolen lands, full rights for land-based peoples.

I ride my pinto into the badlands. I have just heard about the Zapatistas on the radio. Suddenly, like a bolt, I awaken to their brilliance: they have acted on the day that the North American Free Trade Agreement opens the continent to a corporate free-for-all that will, once and for all, destroy land-based sustainability.

1994 Mexico: the economy collapses. Mexico: the economy is propped up.

1995 GATT becomes the law of the Earth.

It is not that you and I were overrun by democracy before; it is not that we had a say in what government or corporations did to the air and water, to the wolves and owls, to our lives.

Malls, clear-cut, fallout.

But now, over roast beef and coffee, the banks and transnational corporations construct the legal right to override any environmental protection, any worker-safety regulation, any human-rights legislation that we struggle to pass. Government subsidies to sustainable farming and community-based technologies are outlawed. The "will of the market" rules.

I am a cardholder.

Where is justice? The World Trade Organization adjudicates all disputes. In its courts there is no guarantee of impartiality, no outside appeal, no media or citizen-witnesses allowed, no disclosure of conflict of interest.

Carte blanche.

1995 Indonesian workers get 15¢ an hour to assemble racing shoes that cost Nike $5.60 to manufacture. You buy them for $135.[16] The company makes $800 million a year. [17]

Seventy-five million people are forced by poverty to leave their native lands in search of work.[18]

The Earth reaches the limits of its capacity to provide resources for the race. The Earth becomes incapable of absorbing the toxins produced.[19]

Two hundred religious leaders pray to Allah, Jesus, and Shakti — raising their crosses and prayer wheels in opposition to corporate ownership and engineering of life.

1997　Asia: the economy collapses. Thailand, South Korea, and Indonesia go bankrupt.

1998　Riots erupt in Indonesia. World financial markets plunge.

Nairobi, Kenya, and Dar Es Salaam, Tanzania: car bombs raze U.S. embassies killing 224 and injuring more than 5,000.

1999　The urge to freedom erupts.

Farmers-against-junk-food drive a bulldozer into a McDonald's restaurant in Millau, France.

Seattle. 50,000 protesters, puppeteers, anti-corporate and pro-localization activists shut down World Trade Organization meetings, causing the talks to collapse.

(Snowflake Martinez rides up the mountain to meet his fellow land grant heirs in a musty pine cabin. They come together to mount a movement for the return of their ancestral lands.)

2000　Prague. 10,000 activists take to the streets to protest IMF and World Bank policies.

2001　Montreal. Seven McDonald's are attacked. Another is destroyed by fire in Tucson.

How it will be.

September 11. New York City. Two commercial airliners hijacked by knife-wielding Middle Easterners careen into the World Trade Center towers, toppling the skyscrapers and instantaneously entombing some 4,000 people. A third hijacked plane is flown into the Pentagon in Washington, D.C., killing 190. A fourth, destined for the White House, crashes into a field in Pennsylvania killing all aboard.

From a cave hide-out in the mountains of Afghanistan, the fundamentalist Islamic organization Al Qaeda demands that the U.S. stop dominating the Arab world for oil profits.

The U.S. pummels Afghanistan with bombs.

How it is.

At home, Americans madly wave the red-white-and-blue. The new U.S.A. Patriot Act dismantles citizens' rights to jury trials and defines "terrorism" as any form of protest or civil disobedience.

How it will be.

A U.S. biotechnology corporation gets the jump on everyone else in a race of its own: it clones a human embryo.

On the map:
YOU ARE HERE.

WHAT IS GLOBALIZATION?

By acquiring earth-spanning technologies,
by developing products that can be produced anywhere
and sold everywhere, by spreading credit around the
world, by connecting global channels of communica-
tion that can penetrate any village or neighborhood. . .

— Richard Barnet and John Cavanagh, *Global Dreams*

CYBER-MAP

*The coming electronic age is the technological
equivalent of Columbus setting sail for the new world.*

— Shelly Schwab, "A Revolution in Television"

In which the map is altered. In which the gold-etched designs with their tall ships and roaring lions disappear from sight. Even the opaque maps of the classroom fade into obsolescence.

New maps are made, state-of-the-art, lines and numbers, computer simulation, digital coordinates. A trillionth of a meter, 3 million light-years away. Cyberspace curved space 750 Kilobits per second — measuring, modeling, predicting; print-out the world the Earth the universe. The making of maps, it is something different; the making, it is something the same.

My first understanding that new maps are on the way occurs in 1969. I have graduated from the University of California at Berkeley. I have protested the war at the Oakland Induction Center, on campus, in People's Park. I have joined the Third World Liberation Strike, nurtured the beginnings of the second wave of the women's movement, been jailed at Santa Rita Detention Center. And I have sat at the Café Med in my beret (rose-hips tea in hand) debating politics, throwing the *I Ching*, reading Frantz Fanon, Krishnamurti, Eldridge Cleaver, Simone de Beauvoir.

I live in a commune on Vine Street. Where the television set comes from that day in July I will never know. But it appears and is placed on the kitchen table atop scatters of black-eyed peas and *Berkeley Barbs*. The appearance of a man in a puffed silver suit bouncing across the black-and-white screen means little to me. It seems distant from our fervent attempt to end American imperialism in southeast Asia. And it certainly does not lend itself to the disturbing medical symptoms of my body shrieking the repressed damage of a childhood of torture. I know there are people whose imaginations are riveted by the moon walk. I know also that there are people who believe that the landing is a media hoax. To me, it represents a crossing to new terrain — against the backdrop of tragedy on planet Earth, terrain with little meaning.

Here to there: *scale and distance*. The map construes the space.

Satellites hurl through it, their telescope cameras and remote-sensing robotics detecting and measuring everything from ozone in the atmosphere to license plate numbers on parked cars in Mexico City, filling computer memories with billions of bits of data. 00100010 01010100 01101000 01100001 01110100 the first words spoken on the moon 00100111 01110011 00100000 01101111 01101110 encoded in zeros and ones and then translated back into English by computer. One small step 01100101 00100000 01110011 one giant leap.

Satellite *Landsat*. Scale: humongous. Distance: unearthly far. Its documentations are maps and photographs at the same time. They speak the age-old cartographic vernacular of hill and valley, river and lake, and yet they reveal not just the lay of the land. Formulated from data fed through remote-sensing instruments, then categorized by computer, they display how the land is used, what grows there, whether the soil is arid or wet, the placement of houses, the makeup of roads, how deep the waters run.

Satellite *Seasat*. It bounces radio waves off the ocean surface. In a single day, 150,000 surface-wind measurements are recorded. These mathematical data are translated by computer into maps, in lines and colors, of the wind's speed and direction over every ocean in the world.

The map construes the space: the whole of the Earth. Some people hail the achievement as a harbinger of unity and peace. And yet totality beds down dangerously close to totalitarianism. Eight-five percent of the planet. Rochester. Forest. Delphos. Fort Wayne. Nothing of this whole Earth is unknown; everything is put to use.

Despite the devastation wreaked by a C minus on my papier-mâché Scotland, I am placed in what is called special math. The class is held in Mr. Anderson's room, way up the back stairs over the girls' gym in what seems a special room. We are the special students, chosen for this hush-hush program because of our grades and leadership abilities. We learn that the decimal number system zero to nine is not absolute. We construct systems based on denominations other than ten, most especially the binary system zero to one. We play with the assumptions behind mathematical systems. We are not told why we are doing these things, only that we are honored to be doing them. We are, it turns out, the first generation of children singled out to think for the computer.

I wonder now who funded the program. The year is 1960. Already the academic-military-industrial complex is solidly in place. Already Princeton's John von Neumann has outlined the critical elements of a computer system. Already AT&T's Bell Laboratories has invented the transistor that will miniaturize electronic circuitry so that computers can be smaller than the massive UNIVAC we have seen on TV. Already scientists, hailing from both academia and the corporate world, have developed the integrated circuit, or computer chip. Already the Soviet Union has launched Sputnik.

The class is easy for me. Yet I am unhappy working inside a junior encapsulation of what, just the year before, C. P. Snow has termed "the culture of the scientific revolution." I want passionately to be with the cheerleaders and school newspaper writers and the hoods who hitchhike and smoke cigarettes outside Standard Drug.

(Snowflake and I have ridden together for half a day. The terrain we have traversed is open and unmarked. With the sky reaching into infinity above us, it has not been important to say whose land we have passed through.

Or perhaps it cannot be said.

The notion of owned earth originates in maps with their straight lines Latin-Long Mercator, boxing what are the boundless pulsations of breath and blood and grasses in the wind. This tenet of the species in possession of place is foreign to the human heart. Passing through, yes. Participating in, caring for, of course. Owning? Let us reflect.

The question is: what place can a people legitimately call home?

The land grants themselves, with their documented boundaries, already represent a cartographic translation into a way of thinking that is questionable against the question at hand. Snowflake has told me that, at one time, straight-line boundaries did not exist. The United States Forest Service and urban tourist-hikers would not know it, but even today the mountains are divided into traditional hunting grounds, grounds with no signs and no fences, places whose boundaries are named by nature, recognized by communities, and can only be known from father to son.

"We hunt in one part of the forest," explains Snowflake. "There are other parts for the Indians at Nambé y other ones for the Tesuques. Pero we would never go in their places."

"Are there fences? Signs?"

"No." He has never before had to think about this or put it into words. "We know the hunting places by water y hills y pictures on the rocks."

What place can a people call home? Even the land grants are modern means etched into existence by imperialism's obsession to define, and yet not far beneath their parchment words, they represent an older way, a way that reaches back into the uncharted annals of human experience. A people may call a place home when they respect the passage of hawks, the overflow of water from the rain-filled river, the ways of other peoples on the land. A people may call a place theirs when they pass through it like generations of elk. A people's place becomes questionable when it is defined by straight-line mappings, military maneuvers, exchanges of cash, and formulations of data that only dimly represent hawks and water and elk.

Snowflake unties his bandana. His face disappears into a blanket of orange as he wipes his forehead. Then he sighs and turns to me.

"We are here."

Empires must continually posture and fight for control of land. World War II could have been predicted: 85 percent of the Earth is already claimed, and the forces that do the claiming are already in collision. Computers are invented to address the complexities of scale and distance endemic to such a global undertaking. They are invented in the only way such a capital-heavy scheme can be — through the consortium of need, finance, and brains called government, business, and academia.

Poland's secret service manages to construct a replica of a primitive German apparatus and smuggle it to Britain. The Enigma is an electromagnetic teleprinter that scrambles messages into codes decipherable only by the plug patterns, or programs, inserted into the machine.

The Z_3 is the first operational computer. It is built in 1941 and, based on the binary system, is designed to solve engineering problems of missiles and aircraft. The German government pays for the work. In 1942, its inventor, Konrad Zuse, and his associate Helmut Schreyer propose that they redesign the Z_3 using vacuum tubes instead of electromagnetic relay switches. Vacuum tubes facilitate the flow of currents by electrical forces alone, using no moving parts, and so function a thousand times faster. The German government pulls the money: it is sure Germany will win the war before the machine is finished.

Meanwhile, British intelligence sequesters a group of researchers in a Victorian estate near London. Their product, inspired by the Enigma, is a code-breaking computer with 2,000 vacuum tubes — coincidentally, the same number Zuse and Schreyer propose for the device they never get to build. This is the Colossos. Intercepted enemy messages are fed into it as symbols punched onto a loop of tape. The tape is fed into a photoelectric scanner that compares the ciphered message with known Enigma codes. The machine processes 25,000 characters a second.

In Endicott, New York, with the navy's blessing and the International Business Machine Corporation's money, a Harvard mathematician named Howard Aiken builds the Mark I. The year is

1943. In this machine, simple electromechanical relays serve as on-off switching devices for the flow of electricity, and punched tape supplies instructions for manipulating data. Unlike his contemporaries across the ocean, Aiken does not grasp the advantage of the binary system which, because it uses only two numbers, simplifies the switching of relays and so quickens the flow of information. The Mark I's data take the form of coded decimal numbers zero to nine fed in on IBM punch cards. The Navy immediately leases the machine to solve ballistics problems. In one day it can whip through calculations that formerly took six months.

Meanwhile, also in 1943, the United States Army unloads hundreds of thousands of dollars onto the University of Pennsylvania's Moore School of Engineering. The task: to build the Electronic Numerical Integrator and Computer, or ENIAC, to prepare artillery firing tables for gunners in the field. The 30-ton result is fearsomely complex, bearing no fewer than 17,000 vacuum tubes. Yet its completion at World War II's end means there is no more need for artillery tables. 18 feet high, 80 feet long, 1,000 times quicker than the Mark I — ENIAC is given a new job: to calculate the feasibility of hydrogen weapons for the Cold War.

To strengthen civil society for this new standoff, the Allied governments release their fancy new machines from military assignment into commercial proliferation. The first computer owned by a business for its own use is LEO, the Lyons' Electronic Office. The year is 1951. It calculates the weekly payroll for a chain of English teahouses.

North south east west: *direction*. The map lays the way.

The psychic pain of living at 2505 Edgehill Road begins with the paternal assault, spreads to include the obscene absence of response from my mother, and comes to encompass the unbearable entanglements of terror, suffering, withdrawal, and loss of esteem passed between my brother and myself.

My departure takes the form of an airplane ticket. The year is 1967. I have saved up $150, and the flight from Cleveland to San Francisco costs $75. West seems the logical direction to head, not just because we Americans are invariably called to go west, but now because the radios are serenading my distress with singular promise: "When you come to San Francisco," they are crooning, "be sure to wear a flower in your hair."

I arrive to my new life with $75 in my pocket, a suitcase carrying the obligatory bell-bottoms and sandals, and a daisy in my hair. I happen upon a free apartment off Euclid Avenue in Berkeley, empty for the summer, and a governess job that pays $12 a day.

I am safe for the first time in my life.

But in this place of no seasons and no family, in the anonymity of morning fog, I am empty. I do not know where I am.

There is no direction inside a computer. Up down north south east west the sun rises the sun sets — the directives humans have known and used for 3 million years of evolution are gone, obliterated by the silicon chip. Stars burst forward like tiny messages from outer space, fly toward us, and then burn up in the blackness of proximity. The silicon chip is built one layer at a time, a skyline city more minute than your smallest fingernail. It controls your car engine. It researches the human genetic map and, from outer space, determines the median income of your neighborhood and the exact locale of terrorist encampments.

For cartographic documentation the chip, with its 3 million transistors, is 100 times more responsive to light than photographic means. It takes as few as ten photons to shoot a picture on a chip, as many as 300 on a photographic plate. What would require two hours to gel on an exposure will emerge on a chip in a few minutes.

Radar. Thermal sensing. Digital lenses. The chip is shooting billions of bits of data through its circuits, arranging them according to predetermined categories. Air quality. Ocean depth. Ocean dumping. Interstate travel. Arctic melt. Guerrilla activity. Desertification. Deforestation. Nuclear tests. Animal migrations. The pilgrimage to Mecca. The march of environmental refugees from one toxic place to another.

Everywhere there is no there. No up. No down. Where inside a computer do the Christmas mailing lists come from? How does a CD player pick out the song you request? How do you fix a broken circuit board? *Where is cyberspace?* The lives of the people whose direction is mapped by computer are severed into digital infinity, everywhere and nowhere at once, the ultimate dream of the imperial mind. "There Will Be a Road," chants the MCI ad. "It Will Not Connect Two Points. It Will Connect All Points. . . . It Will Not Go from Here to There. There Will Be No There, There."[1]

It is not the decolonization movements following World War II that blur the known coordinates and boundaries. Their goal is to reclaim place and identity outside the imperial thrust. The eager and very conscious restructuring of the global economy is what changes things. The men who meet over beef and coffee at the Mount Washington Hotel are pragmatists: they want to create new institutions that will foster their continued control of land, people, and resources. They are idealists: they believe they are building the containers for betterment.

The containers for betterment scorn the solid boundary lines that postwar treaties and agreements lay down. Money becomes stateless. Corporations expand beyond national identity. New technologies like satellites and supercomputers make possible the communications and cash flow necessary for the expansion. As their land and rights are reduced, self-sufficient communities fall to dependence on the cash economy. Everywhere local identity gives way to corporate monoculture. The Wal-Mart in Cleveland is exactly like the Wal-Mart in Guadalajara, Banana Republic in New Orleans replicates Banana Republic in Toronto, Sao Paulo's United Airlines is indistinguishable from Tokyo's.

The scale of these changes is global, the force of their direction irrepressible. Television and social science focus our attention on the new things we can own (automatic garage-door openers South African diamonds laptops phone systems entertainment centers), the places we can go (Tahiti India the moon), the ways we can get there (747 RV space shuttle cyberspace), constantly inserting the idea that progress is here being made.

(The afternoon sunlight feathers its way onto the cabin roof through the needles of a ponderosa as old as the Treaty of Guadalupe

Hidalgo. Snowflake pushes himself up from the rock, and the sun two-steps across his buckskin chaps. He unfastens the buckle and drops the chaps to the ground. Underneath he is wearing jeans made threadbare-blue by a season of mending fences.

I stand up beside him, and despite our most fervent effort to set our toes lightly onto the steps leading to the cabin, our arrival is punctuated by a footfall as clunky as that of my Dutch ancestors in their wooden shoes.

We crack open the door. It is dark, almost damp inside. The inner walls are the same pine logs that form the outside, patched here and there with mud, and the brick floor is covered by swatches of orange shag. There is a window with no glass.

Some thirty men and women, mostly men, are sitting on wood chairs in a semicircle facing a fireplace, looking like a television ad for Levi Strauss. One man stands at the front, and he is talking. I notice something. On the stone ledge before the fireplace sits a very moth-eaten stuffed fawn. It has two heads.

Snowflake shrinks down so as not to appear intrusive. We snake toward the back of the room and find our places on a thick old table, cowboy boots dangling above the shag orange.

"We have pain en nuestra cultura, dolor de la bolsa," the man is saying. Snowflake leans over and whispers in my ear, "This is Tomás. El jefe de la land grant."

"Así es," injects a short, round-bellied man sporting a Burger King T-shirt. "The real merced went away. They left us with only enough land to grow rattlesnakes."

"Lo que dice es como es," chimes in a white-haired vaquero whose blue eyes blaze transparent against his dark skin. "I will tell you. It was years ago. Mi abuelo was taking me to the monte to get a lamb for dinner. We were riding down. I was on my pony. Mi abuelo had the lamb slung over the back of his saddle. Y here comes La Floresta. La Floresta was a new thing, ¿qué no? Before, la tierra era libre. Pero cuando vinieron los norteamericanos, todo cambió. El americano told us to prove the lamb was ours. Pues, there was mi abuelo's brand right there on the skin. Pero La Floresta doesn't believe. He takes the lamb and rides away. Entonces no tiene mi familia nada para comer."

Snowflake leans toward me again. "¿Do you see?" he insists. "The down-to-earth people are finishing."

Indeed, a mighty sadness is hovering in this sierra cabin. It is as if Dolor herself has entered through the door and is serving up burritos de tristeza.

Someone coughs.

Then an older woman with a waist-length silver braid rises from her chair. The silence of the last moments suddenly seems a raucous time. She steadies herself clutching the back of the chair in front of her.

"Creímos que todo que sabemos es de los americanos y sus libros. No viene de la gente ya nada más, ¿qué no? Pero la gente knows everything we need. ¿Recuerdan ustedes cuando hacían leña, do you remember when we went for wood? If you put green wood in the wagon, it killed the horse, ¿qué no? If you came back with twigs, everyone laughed, '¡Tienen el nido del cuervo!' Pero si you came back with la leña blanca, toda la gente andó alrededor del carro con aprobación y tal vez un poquito de envidia."

Haltingly she sits back down.

The man in the Burger King T-shirt follows her lead, standing up to speak. "We cannot stop remembering. Lo bueno y lo malo. La merced empezó in the 1700s when la gente came to this place. The boundaries were marked con shrines y mojoneras y dibujos en las piedras. Cada merced is just big enough to provide for la gente, ¿qué no? ¿Qué es La Mesa de las Escobas? Es el lugar donde you get your grass for brooms. You need places with clay to get your roof. You need trees for vigas y latias. You need to hunt y fish y get the medicines. You need all these things in a land grant."

"Entonces vinieron los norteamericanos," spouts a voice from the back arc of the circle.

"Sí, sí. El Tratado de Guadalupe Hidalgo assured us we are keeping the land grants. Pero then came the surveyors y the Court of Public Land Claims, y our merced shrank from 40,000 acres to 7,000. Then in 1915 came La Floresta. They took our land grant del todo. They put it inside the national forest. Ever since, los americanos of one streak or another are telling us what to do or not do with our land. La Floresta is giving it to the big companies, y they take everything they want. Water. Copper. Trees. We end up without."

"Somos presos de la historia," says a man in a handwoven vest. "¡Y ahora somos presos de los environmentalistas!"

"Sí. We fought the big companies out, y now are coming the énviros." Oddly, given the convention of emphasizing the second-to-last syllable, he gives emphasis to the first. "Y the énviros," he says, "they are telling us with their lawsuits not to hunt or fish or gather firewood or cut vigas or do nothing except let them hike. They treat us like their grandfathers did. On top of it all, they are making up stories about us so people think we are stupid."

"Al fín," adds someone, "they want us — no lie — to work those computadores."

Tomás is listening. He paces back and forth, occasionally stopping to adjust his ear to a particularly crucial statement. He is about fifty years old and, in his life, has witnessed the greatest transition this land has known since the volcanoes. He has seen the days of threshing wheat by goat hoof, and he has seen the coming of nuclear weapons and Afghani — and then Mexican and Colombian — heroin. Despite the stresses of the onslaught, he is a thoughtful man, a man of sight and care.

"Tenemos un dolor profundo, we are hurting, ¿qué no?" he says. "¿Qué será nuestra dirección, mi gente?")

When I graduate from Berkeley, no one in my class seems to know where they are going, and I especially. At least my peers, in their directionlessness, have places to go. They go underground to escape federal charges for protesting the war. They flee to Canada. They apply to graduate school. They hitchhike across the continent from Vermont to California, from California back to Vermont. They get married, get jobs, have babies. They get airline tickets to Nepal.

But I am going nowhere. Begins a twenty-year stint of post-traumatic stress that appears to the myriad surgeons and doctors, acupuncturists and herbalists as pelvic inflammatory disease, not as pelvic inflammatory disease, as endometriosis, not as endometriosis, as *Candida albicans*, not as *Candida albicans*, as depression, not as depression, as environmental illness, not as environmental illness.

It is a tedious twenty years. My childhood has been robbed. Now my young adulthood is sapped. I find my groping way into the world of alternative medicine blossoming in the northern California hills. One thing is certain: I have within me a bottom-line urge to track problems to their source, and so I give unswerving attention to each social change effort as it erupts. Each one texturizes the soul of a period of my life; each one teaches me another facet of imperialism: its racial practices; its wars, the truncation of women's and men's places within it; pesticides and preservatives; the body/mind split; weapons of mass destruction; exploitation of the land; economic inequity; the repression of intuition, sensuality, and spirituality; the erasure of knowing. My urgency to peel away the layers of repressed memory to the source of my own illness propels me to excavate the layers of illness of the society that causes child abuse in the first place.

It is not a recognized or popular direction.

This and that: *detail*. The map names what is.

What is globalization? Details become available.

The full Earth is seen from *Apollo 17*, the last journey to the moon, December 1972, from a distance of 23,000 miles. It looks like the blue-green marble you would trade for all the other marbles, even the cat's-eyes. Africa is visible in its entirety. Also visible are most of Antarctica, the Arabian Peninsula, Iran, a portion of India, as well as the western half of the Indian Ocean and portions of the Atlantic. The sky is clear over the Sahara Desert to the north and the Kalahari to the south.

The full Earth is seen by the World Trade Organization from the distance of a computer screen. You can see the Coca-Cola factory in its entirety. There is most of General Electric, Times Mirror, Union Carbide, and a branch office of Intel, as well as the western half of Matsushita and the travel lanes of Exxon. The sky is polluted over American Express to the north and Cargill to the south.

These details are crucial for us to understand. What once was a forest community, a seaside village, a river people thriving without need for food or tools from elsewhere, is now inundated by McDonald's and Taco Bell, GTE and Hilton. Who once were people connected to each other, community, and the natural world are now fractured by previously nonexistent social problems and, in their confusion and pain, called stupid.

There are many details that are not available. Who makes the decisions that propel IBM and Sumitomo? How do corporate executives and government officials collaborate for their mutual benefit? How do the shadow drug-slave-arms trades facilitate the legal economy? What is the relationship between the laws and institutions of this new form of empire and the economic, social, psychological, and spiritual problems of our lives? What rights that we have exercised in the past are now being eradicated? What plans are being mapped, without our input, for the future?

Detail: my father is staring out the window of the nursing home where he lives his last days. He is ill from multiple sclerosis, alcoholism, and the perpetration of evil. The rural sanitarium he has run for years will be sold at the bottom of the barrel, he tells me, and a developer's dream one-stop high-rise apartment complex/supermarket/bowling alley will rise in its place. He personally will not benefit from the development. And yet, over his milk-protein drink, he smirks, "That's progress."

Progress.

Or rape.

The global economy is everywhere. Computers are everywhere. And the people who rely on them to link themselves to life become everywhere faceless placeless. The details of the demise of the land are everywhere evident. Now the people are strutting in puffed-up pride because the very technologies that cause the demise can also document it.

My father sighs one last raspy breath in his metal hospital bed.

Scale and distance. Direction. Detail.

The new maps are sadder than the human heart can tell.

BANANA-REPUBLIC SUPERHIGHWAY

The Global Information Infrastructure offers instant communication to the great human family.

— Al Gore Jr., "Technology Democracy"

So many roads. So little time.

— Dodge advertisement, 1997

To the global mind, the information superhighway is the route to the unified world. Find it in cyberspace: get your corporate headquarters (and credit cards) there in a nanosecond. To the imperial mind, venues of virtual arrival become invitations to binary supposition, announcements of presumption devoid of sight or caring.

The story on TV is that a scraggly but excited villager in Asia is calling his émigré relative in the United States with a plastic phone card. The story is that children in inner-city Philadelphia are bright-eyed, bushy-tailed talking on computers to children in India. By gosh, you have a keypad pal in South Africa! The world has arrived, with all the glory of its diversity, into techno-oneness.

And we have the global information infrastructure to thank. With its lasers beaming through space microwave satellite to dish, with its glass wires running to every location, the penetration is invisible, the glimpse more consummate than the carvers of Der Rom Weg could ever have envisioned. The tract is neither carved in wood nor etched on parchment; it resides in the ethers of cyberspace.

What is superhighway. Multiplex. Virtual. Hypercapable. What is seamless web of computers, databases, communications networks, and consumer electronics that is changing the way we live. Fiber optics harboring millions of linkages over a single strand of glass.

What is. That expedites the way transnational corporations flash capital from one corner of the planet to the other. That demolishes company towns with a finger to the delete key. That uproots workers from their families, turns land-based cultures into Club Meds. That stunts all possibility of existence outside its definition of survival, gives mail-order catalogs seats at the United Nations. Sustainability becomes not connection to wind, land, and ancestors. It becomes how well business and government maintain the conditions that perpetuate the race.

Albert Gore Sr. It is the 1950s, and the senator is the champion of the interstate superhighway. Not only will a national highway system link every place in the United States with every other place — Gore is breathless as he addresses his colleagues — it will reduce auto accidents, boost employment, and provide the country with the means for military defense. I remember. As a child, my mother and I take the rapid transit downtown. Or we drive straight down Euclid Avenue. As a teenager, both train and avenue suddenly become too slow. Now anyone with a map and a Chevrolet snakes along Liberty Boulevard to the interstate, shoots around the cloverleaf (past the cocked Nike missile), and swoops into downtown from behind Public Square.

Albert Gore Jr. It is the 1990s, and the vice president is the champion of the information superhighway. He espouses a network of communications technologies that will link every person in the United States, reduce auto accidents, boost employment, and aid military defense. Gore is not shouting. He is not a breathless kind of man. But the vision causes others to lose their breath. Fiber-optic cable bundle of microwaves, they are heaving, the links will go everywhere.

Even backward. Seated before a high-resolution color monitor, you are "sailing" the veritable course of Cristóbal Colón: a zigzag of straight-line segments crossing 14,000 digital coordinates that represent the coastlines of over 300 Caribbean islands and the boundaries of 200 shallows. Welcome to the Columbus Research Tool, cyberspace's answer to the centuries-old debate about which New World island Cristóbal Colón first encounters.

Over the years no fewer than nine landfall islands have been proposed, justified, and breathlessly debated — Cat, Conception, East Caicos, Egg, Grand Turk, Mayaguana, Plana Cay, Samana Cay, Watling. The earliest favorite is Cat Island, supported by American essayist Washington Irving. In 1825, historian Martín Fernández Navarrete opts for Grand Turk. In 1882, Abraham Lincoln's assistant secretary of the navy, Captain Gustavus Fox, concludes that, without running afoul of logbook descriptions or the layout of coral reefs, Colón's route could end nowhere but Samana Cay. Then, in 1942, Admiral Samuel Eliot Morison declares, "[T]here is no longer any doubt. . . . I consider the question settled once and for all and in favor of Watling Island."[1] In 1986, though, *National Geographic* editor Joseph Judge defies Morison's certainty.

He does so with a computer.

Now here's an adventure! Electro-whizzes Carla Ryti and Scott Devitt create the Columbus Research Tool, an interactive program installed on a Control Data 170/865 with a digital display of the geography of the Bahamas. Judge's friends Luis and Ethel Marden join up. He invites them not only for their travel experience and mathematical expertise but, Columbus buffs that they are, because they have already attempted to reproduce the transatlantic voyage on their own ketch.

Using two personal computers, a Tamaya NC-77 and NC-88, the Mardens calculate what has never been brought into the equation: the likely effects of ocean currents and the sideways skid of the vessel due to wind pressure against the hull and sails. With this never-before-considered data, the Columbus Research Tool plots all the proposed and conceivable routes and matches them against the

logbook descriptions. What emerges is a moment in the history of
exploration of import equal to the race to the headwaters of the
Nile. Or the ragtag arrival at the Pacific Coast. Or for that matter,
Cristóbal Colón's anchorage itself. Joseph Judge proclaims that the
real landfall is not Watling Island. There is no doubt this time: it is
Samana Cay.

("We need to study los mapas, Oso." Tomás looks to the man in the
Burger King T-shirt. He does in fact resemble a bear, a cross
between a fierce black grizzly from the monte and a cuddly oatmeal
teddy from 100 AKER WOOD.

A frozen gasp locks across Oso's face. "¡Aaaaa-iiiiii! No los tengo.
Creo que I lost them en El Cañón de las Piedras." A ripple of impa-
tience passes through the cabin. "Volveré, volveré." Oso is sweating.
"I will find the maps." Insofar as a spherical body can, he bolts from the
cabin, jumps onto his horse, and rides into the forest.

The group pours out of the cabin. Snowflake hesitates, seemingly still sensitive to his position as a latecomer, and we are the last to
pad down the steps. Standing among the horses, the men pass
around GPC cigarettes. The women arrange themselves against the
bark of a fallen snag.

"Snowflake, bro." The man with the ice-blue eyes offers his hand,
and the handshake that follows extends into time and space like an
elaborate performance piece. "Mambo." Their palms lock together
with the sound of air sucking out of a vacuum-packed Maxwell
House can. "Primo." Their hands slide apart like the bodies of tango
dancers. "Primo." They fix into a final clutch of buckled fingers.

"This is my friend Che."

Mambo rivets every cell of his casindio being onto what is left of
my femininity after four hours of saddlework, and I practically fall
into the blue of his eyes. "Con mucho gusto." He takes my hand in
a European-style clasp. "It is too bad we are not with the electric
highway, ¿qué no?" He smiles broad and white. "We will not have to
wait for Oso anymore."

At this very moment, Snowflake glances down to his boot.
There at the toe, with all the serendipity of the forest, appears a

dust-clotted jumble of red, green, yellow, and blue plastic-covered copper wires lashed together by a tattered supermarket twist tie. "¡HA! ¡Oso doesn't have to go anymore!" He picks up the paltry promise of prewireless electronic confluence and dangles it before our faces. *"Frijoles superhighway."*)

After forging strategic highways into Mexico, the United States government usurps well over half of that country's land base. It feigns help to Cuba in the fight against imperialist Spain, then implants its own militarized monocrops. The nation seizes Hawaii, Puerto Rico, Guam; engineers a revolution against Colombia; constructs the state of Panama so it can build a canal. It inserts soldiers and cash registers in Honduras, El Salvador, Nicaragua. By midcentury many of the previously self-sufficient countries of Latin America have been turned into United States–backed "banana republics:" their lands have been usurped from community-based sustainable uses, carved into privately owned estancias, and are cranking out tons of bananas and coffee for the profit of United States corporations.

"United Fruit Inc. / reserved for itself the juiciest, / the central seaboard of my land," writes Chilean poet Pablo Neruda in a poem damning foreign exploitation and revealing the complicity of local despots;

> *it alienated self-destiny,*
> *regaled Caesar's crowns,*
> *unsheathed envy, drew*
> *the dictatorship of flies.*[2]

"The comprador repressors . . . have raped women in the presence of family members," further details political analyst Michael Parenti,

> burned sexual organs with acid and scalding water, placed rats in women's vaginas and into the mouths of prisoners, and mutilated, punctured, and cut off various parts of victims' bodies, including genitalia, eyes, and tongues. They have injected air into women's breasts and into veins, causing slow painful death, shoved bayonets and clubs into the

vagina or, in the case of men, into the anus causing rupture
and death.[3]

Banana Republic opens on Mill Valley's East Blithedale in 1978. It is
your proverbial hole-in-the-wall posthippie store, and its attraction is
immediate. We have already scoured the army surplus stores in
Oakland for wide-legged navy pants and olive jackets, more often
than not picking up scabies along with street-smart fashion. But these
clothes are the musty moth-eaten stuff of America's recent wars:
World War II, Korea, Vietnam. Banana Republic holds forth an array
of hitherto unavailable items hailing from far more exotic locations:
khaki caps with earflaps to shield the blistering Moroccan sun; linen
jodhpurs donned by British lieutenants perched along the Nile; wick-
er suitcases, leather saddlebags. These are the emblems of the kind of
romantic adventure that has been dangled before us in the films and
literature of the Western world. Swashbuckling soldiers. Aviators.
Gentlemen officers. Wind, sand, stars. Classic, foreign, elite.

Colonial.

We have somehow found within ourselves the sense to see
through Vietnam and the moon shot. But here in the door jamb to
our closets, we fall into confusion, taken in by the potency of the
myths that have molded our collective consciousness. Confession:
before Banana Republic, in a kind of emotional extrication from the
pain of empire, I merely long. After Banana Republic, I embrace.
You will never again find me stripped of a white linen shirt. A pair of
jodhpurs. A World War I leather pilot's helmet.

Banana republic. Panama is a banana republic. Honduras.
Nicaragua. Venezuela. But is a hole-in-the-wall in Mill Valley,
California, the banana republic of the fashion world? The store prolif-
erates, opening a second outlet on Polk Street in San Francisco. It is a
bigger space, five times as big, and yet the exotic-romance theme persists. There are some mass-produced shirts and pants now, the kind of
thing you might don to trek through urban streets to land a cappuc-
cino — but there are also pith helmets and lace-up leather paddock
boots and big-faced watches with khaki bands. Airplanes hang from
the ceiling, and the walls of the outlet are painted like zebra hide.

"Donna?" I am calling my wild friend who lives in a top-floor apartment converted from an old schoolhouse in Brooklyn. "Donna? Is there a Banana Republic on Columbus Avenue in New York?"

"Yes. I'm sure there is. Banana Republic? Columbus Avenue? *Definitely.*"

"Perfect."

Donna treks a respectable length of Columbus Avenue, fifty blocks, from St. John the Divine to Columbus Circle. The Banana Republic outlet is at 69th. The store is a major letdown. Primed by my stories of East Blithedale and Polk, she is hoping for pith helmets and aviator goggles.

"Chellis, there is no more army-surplus."

"Oh."

"They have 360 outlets in Canada and the United States."

"Oh."

"They're owned by The Gap."

"Really."

"They're opening four new 30,000-square-foot retail emporiums."

"Huh."

"Chellis, they're selling the kind of clothes you'd wear to a job in a transnational corporation."

"Oh."

"Almost every item is contracted out to a foreign factory: the Philippines, Turkey, Singapore, Indonesia. I heard that what Levi did for denim, Banana Republic does for khaki. The chinos alone are made in Macao, Portugal, Hong Kong, and someplace called 'United Arab Emirates.' Word has it that they are made in sweat-shops like the textile factories of the industrial revolution."

"Do they still have the photojournalist vest?"

"Yeah. It's made in Thailand."

"Oh."

"You're not disappointed?"

"Well, yes . . . I am. But let's think this through. Maybe there's symmetry here. Maybe Cristóbal Colón and Teddy Roosevelt would still be proud. Dig it, British field boots are a thing of the past; *lap-top wear* is de rigueur for the new colonialism . . ."

(Up the trail treks a lone hiker. Bright-eyed and bushy-tailed would have to be the description. He is a young American dressed REI from head to toe. His PROTECT WILD PLACES T-shirt is slate blue, and he has donned the latest in safari wear, Mondo Cargo shorts. But the crown of the ensemble resides on his feet: a brand spanking new pair of Nike Air Terra Sertigs.

How surprised this young man must be. Alone with his backpack, and he comes upon not a grove of aspens contemplating the coming turn to yellow, not a herd of wild mustangs or a family of elk. No, it is his fate to encounter a stand of vaqueros, hunters, and curanderas who have ever so recently endured the legal and media assault of urban environmentalists. There is no getting around it. The young man is on the trail, and the trail leads to the cabin.

He stops. Everyone freezes. "Hullo. I . . . uh . . . am looking for Rock Canyon."

The silver woman who spoke about wood gathering waves her arm in an easterly direction. "Pa'yá. Down there."

"Tha-aank . . ." His stilted response seems made not so much of politeness as of unease. Just then what could be the source of his discomfort steps forward. It is a dark vato with shaggy black locks held in place by a red bandana.

"¿Are you un environmentalista?"

"Uh . . . I guess you might say I am."

"¿Did you not see the sign?" A handmade billboard, in style not unlike that executed on the front-cover map in *Winnie-the-Pooh*, sits at the base of the trail. It reads: YOU ARE ENTERING THE FRIJOLES LAND GRANT. ONLY HEIRS AND THEIR FAMILIES ARE WELCOME.

Signs are crucial in these parts. The primary strategy employed by the United States Forest Service to usurp the lands in the first place was to put up signs. This fact explains why the villagers place so much stock in burning Forest Service signs to the ground and in erecting signs of their own. One small tidbit too easily overlooked, though, is not just that Forest Service billboards, manufactured assembly-line-style, are immediately replaceable; it is that all government signs are backed by the latest in all-terrain vehicles and Smokey Bears sporting high-tech police weaponry.

"I saw the sign."

"¿Yeah?"

"I . . . uh . . . thought this was public land, . . . er . . . national forest."

"That's the problem."

At this moment, the young man's gray eyes laser to the only other Anglo in the crowd. Everyone follows, turning their faces to Snowflake and Mambo. And me. Snowflake gulps into a throat as arid as the desert. "She is OK," he croaks. "She is for the land grant, y she is against the chain stores."

Tomás steps forward. He seems calmer than anyone else. "This road leads to the cañón you are wanting," he assures the young man. "But please remember, sir, y tell your friends: we do not want any more of this conquering.")

"A navigation system that's so accurate," proclaims the BMW ad, touting its onboard computer charting device, "it can position you almost anywhere on earth to within 11 feet." The Jones Live-Map Meter makes a comeback in the age of computers. "TURN RIGHT!" "AVOID MUDHOLE!" Satellites orbiting at 12,000 miles above the planet transmit data pinpointing the latitude, longitude, and altitude of your location to the car's antenna. The onboard computer retrieves a map of the area from a storage disk and displays it on the dashboard screen. Your exact location appears on the map.

There are no more hostile natives on this road. No more dead buffalo bobbing through the waves. The road lays the way. It veers up, held in place by humongous steel-girded columns. It veers down, twisting back on itself in a cement whorl like a wedding cake. Crown Victorias. Dodge Rams. International eighteen-wheelers. And look: Hung Pham of Honda USA is just now showing off. "Look, Ma! No Hands!" He is careening down Interstate 15 at 55 miles per hour, waving his arms out the window. Tiny magnets embedded in the asphalt hold the magnetized vehicle inside the lane's boundaries. Computers control the speed. A spokesman for the National Automated Highway System Consortium says it's like being driven by a chauffeur.[4]

I am on this road. I am not on this road. The unceasing agony of empire. The desperate lunge from gynecologist to internist, from acupuncturist to naturopath, eating macrobiotic, eating naturopathic, downing blue-green algae, sipping sterilized water — all in hopes of curbing the illness I find neither words nor pictures to describe.

There is pain in my uterus. It is like a stalactite, frozen, hard, scratching relentlessly against the flesh. I have long and unbearable periods now, brown blood, too frequent urination, and a haze of fatigue has settled over my bones.

Then, without warning, it happens. The icicle pierces its frosty sword straight into my womb. Jab! Jab! I leave the Earl Grey half-poured and collapse onto the Indian-print bedspread. Jab! Jab! Jab! I curl inward to cradle my torso. The pain is too overwhelming. I unfurl like a limp thread.

A moment of calm intervenes.

Then JAB JAB! JAB JAB! Oh, icicle! Icicle! Torrent of stabbing, grasping, twisting, sweating, heaving.

Then, inexplicably, peace. I gaze out the window at the acorns.

JAB! JAB! Again! JAB! JAB! JAB! My body writhing in convulsions, belly exposed, legs flung apart — as if at this very moment a rape were being enacted upon my body.

The global automated electronic superhighway is flung before us. We feel it. We do not feel it. Its symptoms are brown blood and a haze of fatigue, and at times they double back to explode in vicious stabs. Columbus Avenue. Army Street. We are writhing inside. Banana republic. Pixel value. As if a rape. www.com.

We do not want any more of this conquering.

SMART APARTMENT

Satellite-generated maps are photographs. They display every detail that can physically be displayed, including homes. And if these homes sport state-of-the-art receptor devices, the satellites hurtling above do not merely take the pictures of them that later hang on their walls. They send binary signals translatable into images on television boxes, voices on earphones, data on computer screens, informing the people in the homes what to think and feel, what to remember and what to forget.

Home: it has always been woman's terrain. Harriet's house on 89th Street, Mimere's on Stillman Road, my mother's on Edgehill. My mother is perched at the kitchen counter sipping Maxwell House black. She radiates awe as she reminisces about her idol Josephine Irwin, who has ridden down Euclid Avenue on a white horse to publicize the struggle for woman's suffrage. She herself pickets for welfare mothers' rights, works to set up a loan fund for women, brings Judy Chicago's "The Dinner Party" to Cleveland.

It is said that the women's movement is the most significant social change effort of the twentieth century. For those who have struggled

119

and fought for women's rights, the insight is welcome. But incomplete. Feminism, when not funneled solely into achievement within the empire, is sister to many relations, from the era's decolonization movements to its efforts for indigenous rights and environmental preservation. I cannot say that the feminist movement is more *my* movement than the others: each eruption of vision and discontent returns me in some crucial way to sight and caring. But the women's movement stands momentous.

The first consciousness-raising group in the commune on Vine Street is disquieting. The year is 1969. Ever so tentatively, lacking common language and common analysis, our little gathering forms its lips around such large concerns as male violence, abortion, powerlessness, woman's voice. I can barely speak. Given the extent of my damages, I cannot afford the vulnerability to admit that I am suffering. Or that, in my unconscious expectation that yet another assault is imminent, I see no future.

The first women's march on the Berkeley campus is also disquieting. Uncharacteristically of me, I watch the ragtag collection of courage that day from the steps of the student union. A marvelous woman named Lisa is marching. She has thrown her pregnant body in front of a policeman's nightstick at the Oakland Induction Center to keep the officer from beating her husband one more time. She loses the child. By contrast, the brand of courage I have come to know is survival by psychological repression. Lisa's out-front grit is as compelling as Josephine Irwin's. And yet, seeing her that day, still I do not join in. Matters between men and women are "personal," I insist. The thought mirrors the command my father has whipped into me: abuse is survivable only if unspoken.

Paralysis breaks into embrace the night I see my first female lead guitarist. By the standards laid out in *Mademoiselle,* she isn't pretty, she isn't sexy. She has crudely cropped strawberry hair and a round little body. But behind her shiny Stratocaster, the woman is *raw power.*

I become a feminist. The process of unraveling my story begins.

(Tomás is taping the maps Oso has retrieved onto the stones surrounding the fireplace. The maps offer a picture of the original parameters of the land grant, marked by riverbed and shrine and pet-roglyph. A young woman taps Tomás on the shoulder and whispers to him. He nods. She turns to address the group. The woman is tall and straight with long black hair. She looks to be in her twenties and is wearing a plaid cowboy shirt, jeans, and tan moccasins.

"My name is Delfina Montoya," she begins with a poise rare for her age. "You may not remember me. I grew up in the village, but I went away to school. I just graduated from the university." A hush ripples through the cabin. "I am the daughter of Lucky and Carmela Montoya, who were killed in an automobile crash on the high road last winter. I am taking their place in the land grant. My grand-mother on my mother's side was Rosa Suazo from Santa Clara Pueblo, on my father's Tranquila Vigil from Nambé. In my family we also trace our lineage to central México. We are Tlascaltecas, originally from the state of Pueblo, taken by Juan de Oñate to work in the silver mines of Zacatecas, then to El Barrio Analco in Santa Fe. In the mid-1700s, we came here." She steps forward. "I went away into the world out there, and I can tell you now what I learned: this place is my home, *our* home. We are made of the trout and the water rushing down the mountain, and there is no one on this planet who can tell us otherwise. They try, the surveyors and the lawyers and the politicians and now these newcomers the environmentalists. But they are wrong."

I scan the cabin from my position on the back table. Every person is as still as a petroglyph.

"And I can tell you something more of what I know. This I learned right here. This my grandmother told me. You and me, we are not simply Spanish conquistadores whose job is to suffer the sins of the fathers. No, history is more complicated than that. We are Tewa, we are Tano, we are Tlasclán. We come from the land, and we know how to live on it. When the Americans came, they did not rec-ognize our pueblos or our roots. But we are indigenous people."

Tomás is sitting next to the two-headed calf on the ledge. His eyes are glistening with excitement. Snowflake is sitting next to me on the table, and I sense he is going to burst.

"We say, 'Mi casa es su casa.' Maybe we say it without thinking, without discriminating. Maybe we say it too much. My father used to tell me he wished the old-timers had not been so nice when the Americans came. Maybe you will think me naive. I haven't been with you for years. But I say we look at Oso's maps and we make a plan. I say we give up our dependence on Los Alamos and Wal-Mart and social services. I say we get our real home back.")

My home cannot be located with certainty. Is it the Río Grande valley, where I have lived for fourteen years? Is it the northern California coast I inhabited for twenty? Ohio, where my family settled for generations? The Connecticut valley, where they arrived in 1635? Is it Holland, Wales, Ireland, Scotland, England, France, Belgium, Germany? The North? The forestlands of the Celt?

My home is a Victorian apartment in Berkeley slated for demolition: 1612 Walnut. It is a $92-a-month flat behind an auto-repair shop in downtown Oakland: 3012 Brook. A hundred-year-old farmhouse in the woods: 31 Montgomery. The tack room of a barn up Willow Creek Road. I am a renegade from the first rung down on the pyramid of imperial spoils, a refugee from family wars, a class traitor. Without family or money or resources, without membership or ownership, I find it almost impossible to make a permanent home. The rent goes up; the building is torn down. And I am ill, always ill.

The one activity that makes sense is to be with the women. Kent. Hallie. Charlene. Susan. Merlin. Sally. Erica. We meet at dawn in a meadow overlooking the Pacific Ocean. The year is 1977. Huge granite rocks jut up from the grass like the menhirs at Stonehenge. We have discovered something crucial: things were not always as they are now. Women were not always held in check by the tyranny of male authority and the terror of violence. Humans did not always plunder the Earth. Organized war is not a given. We have uncovered a truth: women are wild and free; the Earth is our home. There is nothing disquieting about this. We feel it in our bones. Isis. Diana. Hecate. Tara. Brigit. Lilith. Gaia. As the sun rises pink against the dewy chill that winter solstice, we stand together, our feet planted to the soil. We speak of clarity of vision and the power of our circle. We chant together for courage.

We will need courage. It is said that one day humans will build homes on Mars — "colonies" they are called. Yet right now, inside these postmodern data-wired apartments on this degraded planet. . .

Forgive me. You could insist that some folks residing within global corporate "culture" are like Harriet and Frank sipping their Earl Grey on the veranda. At the very least, they are the settlers and, some would say, the colonizers. They sit at their computer stations downing endless tumblers of banana-republic caffeine and smart cocktails spiked with aminoguanadine. When they are hungry, they push buttons and food appears as if they were in possession of a maid. They wolf down cuisine bioteched in the former colonies and engineered in urban factories.

But there is a question I am dying to pose. Please. Bear with me. Could it be that the settlers themselves, and even the colonizers, are becoming *the colonized*? It is a disquieting thought; no one wants to discover oppression — yet I have in my possession information about what future colonization might look like because, for some, it is already so. Look here: Windsor Castle has long since burned to the ground like a U.S. Forest Service billboard, and with the destruction of all those candelabras and white marble statues comes the finale of a veritable template for living. The new template is the computer. Can you see? In the global economy people are meant to arrange themselves, like the natives of a foreign protectorate, to the computer's dictates. As Franklin Saige so cogently puts it, "We are actually being put *inside the machine*."[1]

Home. Maybe it is a high-tech mansion. Maybe one of those concrete-steel-reebar jobs. Or a retro Victorian flat. Whatever, the centerpiece is a set of white plastic boxes sporting white keys and white buttons, mazes of white wires and white telephones. Or perhaps just one metallic box encased in a smart canvas carrying case. Or a chip in the heel of a shoe.

Everything that concerns survival depends on the functioning alignment of these electronic circuits. Using them, the newly colonized find themselves doing what is vital to their dependence on the corporate machine. They make deals with strangers halfway around the planet, gather information about any subject under the sun, move binary data around as if it were logs on the woodpile. They talk to silicon chips, rock out to digital reverberations. They type in dirty fantasies, print out color maps.

How deeply and yet unconsciously they inhale and exhale the breath of empire: technoglobalization is in the air! Just as the lord of yesterday's dominion controls the servant's every move, so the machines tell the newly colonized when to get up, what to wear, how to lift their thighs to achieve a sculptured look. Machines do everything for them from chopping vegetables to reporting their financial options. They are accessorized in wearable chips interlocking them to every electronic device in the house — cell phone, digital assistant, beeper, personal stereo, vacuum cleaner. Socks tagged with sensors inform a readout on the dryer which ones are paired with which, and the great shopping interface provides them with state-of-the-art graphics, consumer reports, and customer complaints for all the latest goods at Harrod's and Mikimoto. If they want, using their virtual interfacing device, they can even feel the pearly spout of a teapot from China.

Well, maybe not. Probably they are in too much of a hurry to be fingering spouts. A perpetual compulsive stressed-out hurry. "Speed of light versus bullet." Computers dictate their schedules, and they need computers to keep up the pace. "In 0.0043 seconds, the entire works of William Shakespeare translated into 200 languages sent from New York to Omaha, Nebraska without skipping a verse."[2] The people are running, worrying, working three jobs at once.

The whole thing is maddening, disorienting, beyond the capabilities of human nerve cells to withstand. And so the newly colonized take drugs. Uppers. Downers. In-betweeners. Tea from India. Coffee from the former colonies. Prozac. Sugar. Codeine. Heroin. Valium. Cocaine.

And they surround themselves with contents. Wide-screened high-resolution television receivers, remote-controlled entertainment centers, high-riding trucks, slick things, new things, expensive things. But also (sometimes) real things: shawls woven by Guatemalan grandmothers, African fertility dolls, spoons shaped like Aztec gods, contents that are distinctly anthropological. And faux. The truth is, the bulk of them have not been crafted for use within their own cultures; they have been manufactured specifically for consumption in the global economy. People in England possess flying frogs from the island of Bali. Folks in the United States decorate their living rooms with santos carved in Peru, miniature statues of the Chinese goddess Quan Yin, Canadian bark chairs.

Look here: perched on these branches from Ontario, I am trying to describe the predicament. But my words only come out twisted and labyrinthian. This is because the predicament itself is twisted and labyrinthian. Everywhere the ground is shifting, the boundaries dissolving. What was once yours is now mine, private becomes public, sacred profane, real virtual, colonizer colonized, settler unsettled. It is a confusing time. American Express, United Airlines, and the CIA are to thank for everything people have, Times Mirror for everything they believe. Like satellites and computers, people's attention seems to be located everywhere at once. "The digital planet," boasts MIT Media Lab founder Nicholas Negroponte, "will look and feel like the head of a pin."[3]

And the people in it no longer remember what they have forgotten. Invisible corporate entities are broadcasting right into their brains. "We'll Never Leave You Alone,"[4] they are crooning, and by God, the admonition defines the very nature of empire. "Imagine a World without Limits Where Anything Is Possible."[5] "Go Farther. Go Farther. Go Farther."[6] "It's All within Your Reach."[7]

Yet, for all the precision of the maps and charts available in cyberspace, few are able to see empire. Blindness is rampant. Denial, repression, outright refusal. And the more that is forgotten, the more that falls away, that dissolves and disappears, the more there is to remember.

("Rosalía, tú puedes recordar." A woman who has not spoken jumps from her chair in the circle. She is middle-aged and looking older than her years. A rotund belly stretches her striped tank top, and the number *23* on it is elongated sideways over her big breasts. "Por favór," she says to the silver-braided elder. "Dínos."

The feel of the cabin shifts. It seems to me that the men, by their sheer numbers, have defined the voice and pacing up to the moment Delfina asks to speak. Now something else is happening, something like birds in formation dipping, diving, rearranging their pattern of flight. Snowflake glances over at me, his black eyes singing with expectation. He juts his lips in the direction of the change.

"Sí, Viola."

Once again the old woman takes a long moment to lift her body from the seat, and once again she steadies herself by clutching the wooden chair at her side. "I remember the things de mi vida. Y I remember what mi abuela told me. Yo tengo ochenta y cinco años. Mi madre was born the year the land grant was given — 1891. Mi abuela was born the year of the Treaty of Guadalupe Hidalgo — 1848."

Everyone in the cabin is as still as a deer listening for its mate.

"Before los norteamericanos y for some time after, women were tough y free more than today. Mi great-grandmother owned her own house. She knew the medicines. She planted, baked bread, dried las frutas y chile y carne. She spun yarn y panned for gold y rode with the men. Y she gambled in the plaza. I will tell you. Mi great-grandmother was known for her dancing at the fandangos. She twirled with her fancy earrings, y when she found out her husband had taken some of her lambs to sell, she threw his clothes on the front step y divorced him flat. Woman's place was the house. Teníamos poder y libertad."

"Es diferente ahora," muses a woman leaning against the table.

"Sí, sí," clamors Rosalía, waving after her with one blue-lined hand. "Es verdad. Despues de que vinieron los norteamericanos, todo cambió. Our people lost our communal lands to the new government, y nosotras las mujeres lost our property to the men. We lost our power. Nuestra libertad was finished when the corsets came."

A silence rises up, and it lasts far longer than it ever could if the men were not hanging back. It is a silence that wraps its presence around every shiny black hairpin and every crusty leather boot in the room. There is no awkwardness in this silence. No. It is comforting, more a settling, a deepening, like a prayer to the unseen forces of the mountain.

Then Viola, who has been sitting on the ledge by the fireplace, clears her throat. "Our job is cut for us," she says. "Our job is to preserve nuestra cultura, nuestras familias, la lengua, la tierra. The men are still fighting the battles outside, y nosotras las mujeres are still at the center."

At this moment Delfina cranes her torso toward the table in the back. "¿How is it for you?"

She is looking at me. My bones freeze. It is honor enough just to be here — but to *speak?* The onus of representing the dominant society drapes my body like an X-ray apron. I am from it and of it. The challenge is to shape a conversation that is not.

"I am listening to you," I begin. My voice seems squeakier than usual. "I . . . ah . . . I didn't know what happened to you so abruptly in 1848. I am just now learning. And I have also been learning that the same things that happened to you happened to my people — abruptly thousands of years ago when our communities in northern Europe were conquered by hostile tribes, abruptly again when the industrial revolution took away what land and rights we still had. But also slowly, over generations and generations, women became private property like land, and we lost our power. What is it like for us? Community is rare. Families are broken. The house is not the center anymore. To work there has become a thing of drudgery and isolation. The same oppression that happened in our world is what my people imposed on you." I pause and look around the cabin. Everyone is attentive, and Snowflake is nodding his head. "Women in the dominant society have long since lost the center. Most of the time we don't even remember that there was a center. We get confused. Do we make ourselves whole again by being successful in the man's world? But isn't the man's world as twisted as the woman's? Maybe we can re-empower ourselves on our own terms? The question is: where is the center anymore?" I am gaining my stride. "I feel inspired when I listen to you. What you know has to do with basic things for women and men everywhere: freedom, dignity, connection to place, survival. When I listen to you, I feel fierce with clarity. I remember.")

Memory: it is 1975. The women are leaving home, bolting en masse. The soldiers, they are coming home, limping, uncelebrated. Passing in the threshold, going and coming, the women and the soldiers put post-traumatic stress disorder on the map.

Shell shock is a condition that fragments and dispels memory. Because of its prevalence among American men after World War I, it momentarily seeps into the civilian mind as a phenomenon demanding attention and then instantly, in an atmosphere pervaded by fright, is repressed. The challenge to the necessity of male bravado for war-making is too daring, the symptomatic memory of battle trauma pressed back into the collective unconscious with no bravado at all.

And now here, off the military transport planes, come the soldiers from Vietnam, a shattered bunch in their jungle fatiques. They too carry the aftershock of war in the cells of their bodies, expressing it again and again in the daybright of a city park, in the dark of a movie house, in the fluorescence of a hospital ward. They are meeting now in storefront vets' centers and rapping about their agonies. They are giving each other the solace that no one else can provide. They are making the rest of the country face the ghastly reverberations of war. And some of them are daring to question the act of imperialism itself. But ultimately not enough veterans find space to rap. Or perhaps it is because the damage is too great. Upon arriving home, more veterans than are killed in battle down bottles of sleeping pills and put magnums to their own brains.[8]

The women are meeting and rapping too. And this intersection of memory is where the interweave of the social act of imperialism with the private deed of rape comes home. In their kitchens and their communes, the women are uncovering the ubiquity of assault upon them. Rape is not sexuality or love, they are saying; it is political repression to enforce subordination. The revelation of widespread sexual assault leads to talk of battery in the home, and this leads to the discovery of the abuse of children. One woman in four is raped in her adult life, one in three as a child.[9]

Home: *this* cannot be woman's terrain. *This* cannot be the place the soldiers are fighting to protect. Home: it is instead a place of frightened flashbacks and murderous revenge, of crazed thoughts and compulsive isolation. It is a place where the traumatized reenact their terrors upon others, where others become the newly traumatized. It is source to the original urge to squelch the spirit of a child, a woman, a man, a people, a land.

"But *my* family isn't like that!" you insist, taking every precaution to lift yourself above the fray. And yet the emotional chaos of the empire is happening everywhere. It is happening next door and in the Malaysian jungle and at the Japanese stock exchange. It is happening to your best friend and to your cousin, to the man with the crack cocaine and to the actress who shops on Rodeo Drive.

Yes, the maps generated by satellite and computer are precise. Now is the time when every detail is being revealed. Every license plate of every vehicle parked on the street. Every tanker transporting toxic waste. Every soldier crashing from his bed in a sweat. It is a time of seeing. Of remembering.

I remember.

Yes. I do remember. What? My guts pulse with unremitting horror and terror. But the sensation attaches to nothing. Wait. A picture flashes.

A child.

A child lying facedown. Horror, terror.

A child at home.

What?

VIRTUAL WILD

*In the closing decades of the twentieth century, reality
is disappearing behind a screen.*

— Howard Rheingold, *Virtual Reality*

Even Mimere's secret garden becomes a bird's-eye plat of false-hue colors. Presumably, somewhere within these bright maps, pachysandra flourishes and morning glories wind up trellises to the sun. But we cannot know. Well, not until we call up the official list of nonextinct flora to a box on the screen.

And please note: the place where leones abound no longer resides at the edge of the European fiat in northeast Asia. It is accessible now only within a head-mounted display that fabricates electronic jungles where vivid yellow cats stalk the human intruder who, in defense, madly pokes buttons and waves about a sensory glove.

But wait: you *can* see nature in person. Almost anyone can pass through a clear-cut forest on the interstate. For a price, you are invited to visit elephants at the animal rehabilitation farm. The true adventurer, though — you in your photojournalist vest — can bob along the Snake River in a dugout canoe, like Meriwether Lewis and William Clark before you, on a packaged reproduction of the original expedition. But please beware: see is what you will do. Distance to scale. It is not required, or even allowed, that you hunt deer or gather herbs for your survival. Bag lunches will be provided. Or if you prefer, you can order a McNugget plate. In the national forest, it is illegal to pick a flower and medical madness to drink water from the stream.

Welcome to the completely imperialized planet. This is virtual wild. If the elaborate gardens at Versailles display the essence of early imperialism's construction of nature, so these simulations-from-unearthly-distances and extinction-tours reveal the end-story meaning of global technoempire.

Indeed, it has long been rumored that the finale is nigh. The obligatory end-of-the-world hysteria born of linear perspective meets its match in the physical world. Sometime in the 1980s scientists proclaim that we have but ten, maybe twenty years to alter the basis of the imperial livelihood; ten, maybe twenty years before the damage becomes too excessive for the Earth to bear. And how, for us poor human beings, could all this shell shock and trauma continue anyway? It, too, is unbearable and, to borrow a phrase from ecology, unsustainable.

The memories are coming fast now. It is summer. I am driven along with my brother and cousin into the woods, a metal building at the end of a country road. My father and his accomplice drag us one by one into the dark of the building. I remember the interminable wait outside among the maples and oaks and the buckeye trees.

The buckeye is very special. In fact, it is designated the official tree of the state of Ohio. Hailing from the horse chestnut family, it boasts extravagant flowers, a cluster of canoe-shaped leaves, and big green burs. Inside the burs reside the nuts, so shiny, so elegant, so reddish-brown they emerge from their spiny habitat like tributes to the perfectly waxed cherry table in Aunt May's foyer.

I remember.

I remember the sand scratching against my back and thighs as my attacker groans and sweats and rams into me. I can see my father's face, and the other faces, as they enforce their moment of dominance. I know these people. They are flesh and blood. They are not like the nut treasures of the buckeye tree, so smooth and gracious in your hand. They are mean and calculating in a way that cannot be fathomed.

I remember camp. "I'm Red Raider born and Red Raider bred!" We are at the lake, I in my frilly bathing suit with the red cherries all over it. The counselor is teaching us to dunk our faces in the water.

But the prospect only reminds me of the time when, at Indian River, my father maliciously holds my head underwater. I go running into the woods. Maple. Oak. Buckeye. "And when I die, I'll be Red Raider dead."

Who, really, would want to be present for such moments? The psyche pushes the experiences into an unlocated sphere of the brain that is specifically designed for *not* being present, and I am left with a host of agonizing pleas for help called symptoms. Interestingly, these symptoms mirror and metaphorize the original events to a T. An hour after I fall asleep, about when my father would creep in to rape me, my heart pounds so fast and hard it wakes me up. I am afraid to put my head underwater. I am terrified I will be contaminated by a contagious disease. And I have endless health problems that center on my reproductive capabilities.

Remembering what lies behind these living metaphors is as terrifying as the original events themselves. It is like pushing over the Bitterroot, beyond Yellowstone, never knowing when a grizzly will appear raised up to full height, eager to gouge your guts out. That which I am incapable of experiencing full-on as a child emerges now like a bear in the woods. But there is a difference. I am not a child navigating grizzly terrain. I am an adult, and I am mature enough to face these moments in all their horror and terror, make sense of their effects, and finally usher them into the past.

Vir: "man" in Latin. *Virtual:* according to the dictionary, "of or relating to a virtue, or efficacious power; as the *virtual* rulers of a country."[1] The Western mode of being is based on the Platonic lifting of real from virtual: the body/mind, Earth/human split. Vir: a man is. Virtual: divided from his own nature, incapable of experiencing, and in agony from the separation, he is *not.*

And so he invents places and expeditions that are. But are not. Why, the inspiration for the nonexistent experience itself emerges as yet another rendition of the Jones Live-Map Meter: virtual reality. The whole planet, after all, has been discovered, mapped, and claimed. There is no more real-world adventure and no more heroic conquest to be had. We are boxed in. But being an ever ingenious

people, and ever insistent on our mode of operation, we conjure up
new horizons.

Hollywood cinematographer and garage inventor Morton Heilig
has a dream. He yearns to produce multisensory experience in arti-
ficial environments. He wants to expand the experience of the
moviegoer from mere observation to visceral involvement, vertigo,
thrill, terror, living breathing knowing. But every time he attempts
to launch his research, his film-industry backers are killed in a plane
crash, they are fired from the positions that would enable them to be
backers, or Heilig himself is fired. Once, World War II intervenes.
He finally builds a small-scale model using the resources of one
small-scale partner. It is a coin-operated pinball-parlor device known
as "Reality for a Nickel."

You sit down in a wooden booth. Suddenly you are riding a
motorcycle through the streets of Brooklyn, circa 1950. You hear
the engine start. You feel the vibration of the handlebars. Wind
blows your hair. You see Brooklyn as it has not looked for decades.
Then Middle Eastern music blares, and a belly dancer is wriggling
toward you clapping her finger cymbals into your ears, emitting the
palpable smell of cheap perfume.

Ultimately, no one with the means to bring Heilig's dream to
reality pays up. It is not until scientists forge breakthroughs in computer development that the dream is made manifest with financial
backing from more reliable sources, not film studios this time but
the Department of Defense. Ivan Sutherland at MIT, funded by the
Office of Naval Research, invents the first three-dimensional head-
mounted display. Daniel Vickers at the University of Utah puts
together the first virtual software image: a wire-framed cube.
Sutherland and his eager colleagues develop the hardware that eliminates all the construction lines of an image that, from a particular
angle, do not need to be seen. NASA scientists are the first to unite
the head-mounted display with the sensory glove. Vickers works on
the pistol-grip wand that allows a person to manipulate images in
cyberspace. Using computer-modeled illusions and three-dimensional visual displays, Myron Krueger pioneers the cyberspace experience beyond the head-mounted screen; he invents whole environments composed of electronic illusion. Michael Naimark and Scott

Fisher build the Aspen Map, a virtual tour of the ski resort town in Colorado.[2]

Once inside cyberspace, you can skip the empire. There are no more angry ghettos. No more forests decimated to the soil. No more violated children. No more rampaging megalomaniacs. No more lies. No more conquering. You step into a world cartoonlike in appearance, and it is so all-encompassing, so controlled, so seductive that you B-E-L-I-E-V-E. Welcome to cognitive engineering. And meanwhile, as you feel thrill and vertigo in this technological wedding cake, governments and corporations are quietly using the same systems to map every last inch of land and ocean on the planet for WTO-sanctioned development. Meanwhile, unbeknownst to you, the military is using computers and virtual reality to design new weapons of mass destruction and even, it is said, conduct psychological experiments that expose people to simulated torture that produces real-life traumatic stress.

Vir: a man is. Virtual: he is not. He snips at what surrounds him. He inserts recombines rearranges edits programs produces. The result: the natural world is. But is not. Here is a potato. A potato, but not a *real* potato, for it harbors the gene of a chicken. Here is an ear of corn made of insects, there a trout with human DNA. Look! It's a sheep sporting tobacco genes. Lo and behold. They've edited a mouse with a human ear growing out of its back! And here is a soybean that is not really a soybean, for it is made of peanuts. Chemists have long since invaded the structure of molecules, passing parts from one substance to another, making them into something they are not. Now bioengineers are invading the makeup of sentient beings, acting like Cristóbal Colón landing on the sandy shores of existence itself. "Go Farther. Go Farther. Go Farther." "We'll Never Leave You Alone."

It all begins when French gardeners clip their hedges to look like pastry, when botanist Joseph Dalton Hooker proclaims colonizing plants to be better than indigenous ones, when heffalumps arrive in England. Here is a frog with no head. It has been created in a laboratory by genetically suppressing development of the tadpole's brain and central nervous system. This is not just a bizarre Halloween prank. Combined with human cloning, it heralds a new scientific horizon. Now you can donate your genes to produce a headless twin who will donate its heart or kidney or liver back to you. Here is a cage full of mice whose ears light up like Christmas trees. "They're cute as can be," boasts Stan Spillman at Stanford University's Molecular Biophotonics Laboratory,[3] describing the injection of fire-fly genes into mouse organs. Look! Some two hundred years past Lewis and Clark's pioneer passage, Yellowstone is under seige. In pioneering fashion, a Swiss corporation mines microorganisms from the geysers and biotechs them to make meat tenderizer.

And here is a tomato. A perfectly good tomato. It is grown in Mexico, and this is both a boon to the economics of the endeavor and a problem for its biology. Days, maybe weeks, are required for the tomato to arrive on your salad. It could go mushy and rotten before you ever smother it in vinaigrette. And so the farmers are instructed to pick the tomato before it is ripe. Green, it does not have the chance to develop its flavor on the vine and arrives all right, but tasting like cardboard.

Along comes FlavrSavr from Calgene, Inc. That's *Cal* for "California," *gene* for "genetic." FlavrSavr inhibits the formation of the enzyme that causes mush and rot. The farmer picks your tomato a few days later than he used to. It is shipped as before, taking days or weeks to arrive, and voilà! It ripens just as it appears on your salad plate.

Renegade biotechnologist Martha Crouch has something to say about this. "The beauty of this solution to the problem of taste-deficient tomatoes," she explains,

> is that nothing else in the system has to change. The tomatoes are grown in the same fields, by the same companies, shipped on the same highways. . . . The problem is answered with a single gene change. However, a company has inserted itself in a new place in the chain. Calgene can now sell the FlavrSavr technology and capture a share of the tomato market profits by having a novel product that it hopes will outcompete other tomatoes. . . . What kind of structure is required to produce and use an industrial tomato?[4]

"I know an old lady who swallowed a Savr," we are crooning at the salad bar:

> *I don't know why she swallowed a Savr*
> *Maybe she'll get some flavr*
>
> *I know an old lady who swallowed a chemistry mill*
> *It singed and smoldered inside her like a poisonous pill*
> *She swallowed the mill to make the Savr*
> *I don't know why she swallowed the Savr*
> *Maybe she'll get some flavr*
>
> *I know an old lady who swallowed a farm*
> *How absurd! How crazed! What alarm!*
> *She swallowed the farm*
> *To pay the mill*
> *That poison pill*
> *To make the Savr*
> *Maybe she'll get some flavr*
>
> *I know an old lady who swallowed the interstate*
> *She didn't want to be late*
> *She swallowed the road*
> *To get to the farm*
> *How absurd! What alarm!*
> *To pay the mill*
> *To make the Savr*
> *Maybe she'll get some flavr*
>
> *I know an old lady who swallowed a power plant*
> *Could she grow a tomato? She cried, "I can't!"*
> *She swallowed the plant to light the interstate*
> *So she wouldn't be late*
> *To get to the farm*
> *To pay the mill*
> *To make the Savr*
> *Maybe she'll get some flavr . . .*

(The maps are U.S.-Geographical-Survey green. Fastened to the fireplace with duct tape, they sit too far away for the group to study them in detail. But there they are, every inch of forest in display textured by red-brown lines of elevation, divided and subdivided into exact little boxes. 36 degrees 7 minutes 30 seconds north. 105 degrees 52 minutes 30 seconds west. We have before us virtual testimony to the land.

Tomás stands up. "Que viva la palabra que está escrita en el papel. We are here today to challenge a la raíz. ¡Viva la justicia! The way things are going — La Floresta giving our trees to the big companies, the ski resorts coming in, your own people making individual claims — this way we have ten, maybe twenty años antes de que we lose everything."

At this moment, the duct tape holding up the village with all its houses and the east-west stretch of mesa, tenderly, as if in slow motion, gives way. The map snaps into a scroll in midair and drops to the shag rug. Delfina jumps up and Mambo too, who is sitting near the fireplace, and with the fanfare of paper rustle that can only be achieved when one is trying to bring order to a map, they gather up the fallen chart and place it on the fireplace ledge.

"Los primeros mapas," continues Tomás, "they are not pictures from the sky like today's maps. In the beginning they are our bodies. We are born to the land. We feel it. We know it. Then, if there is a need to tell someone where is a place, we use words. ¿Do you know El Vallecito en Donde Se Paraba la Gente a Descansar Cuando Iban a Limpiar la Acequia de la Sierra?"

Thirty heads nod in immediate recognition.

"Words are put into the treaty, ¿qué no? Written. With ink. Sacred words. They say that our people own the land up to the heights above the river. They say we have the land that goes all the way to La Cañada de la 'Pacha. Our claim es el Pueblo Anciano, where nuestra gente settled abajo."

"There are people here who remember when los norteamericanos came with los survey people to make the first mapas," comments the man in the woven vest.

At this moment, an older gentleman stiffens his back and raises one plaid arm. "Yo andaba pa'yá. I rode them into the monte."

"Sí. José was there," Rosalía says. "He remembers."

"Sí, sí. Yo andaba pa'yá. Y I took los survey people up to the peaks, la Sierra Luciérnaga, Cerro de la Loba, el Vallecito de la Sierra. Y entonces ellos hicieron los mapas, ¿qué no? Y los mapas were lies. Dicen que la merced es más pobre que es."

"Y entonces viene el gobierno," pipes in Mambo. "Y el gobierno slaps La Floresta onto el monte y todas las mercedes."

I find it curious that the story is told again and again. It seems important, essential, that it be told and retold, every detail placed on display for all to witness over and over again, every facet of the story rehashed and rediscovered in relation to every other facet. I am struck. How many times must these people retell the story of what happened to them? How many ways must they juxtapose and then reconcile the robbery of the lands with the loss of livelihood? The promises with the lies? The violence with the neglect? And how many times must I retell the story of what happened to me? How many ways must I juxtapose and then reconcile the hurt done at the hospital with the rapes in the car? The forced witnessing of my brother's tortures with my mother's relentless absence? The blood pouring from my vagina with the dissociation of a world that does nothing to help? Each time the story is told and reexamined, for me and for the people in this cabin, a new thread is revealed. Each time the meaning sinks to a deeper place in the bone.

Snowflake is vibrating like a rocket revving to take off. "One day last fall," he calls out, "Snap-On y Muelas y yo venimos al monte parar cazar. We were looking for alazán. We rode y rode, por tres días we rode up the monte to a special hunting place. It was snowing y my horse fell on the ice. Snap-On lost his pack, pero we got there. ¡Qué sorpresa! There was a brand new paved road built coming in from the other side of the monte. All of a sudden a bus pulls up. ¡Instead of alazán, órale, we find a hundred turistas from Germany with their down jackets y cameras!"

"What put me to thinking is, if we don't get our land," says Mambo, "we will be turistas, backpackers, environmentalistas ourselves, usando the forest only for . . ." — he scrunches his thick eyebrows ominously — ". . . *fun*."

I glance around the cabin. All the people are staring at the rug and shaking their heads. Tomás sends his sad eyes out the window to the trees.)

~

Tree trail wind/skyscraper freeway exhaust. The urban nature enthusiast has sad eyes too. Climber, backpacker, skier — his athleticism springs from an authentic source. Photographer, flower collector, spirit-seeker — her love for Creation is real. But channeled through the assumptions and demands of a society pitted as it is against the natural world, athleticism and love become truncated expressions severed from their original involvement in communal survival.

You realize there is no such word as *wild*. Not in any language spoken by native peoples, and we can assume that these are the languages that best express who humans evolved to be. No "wild." No division of human from Earth. No hikers escaping civilization. No abrupt reentry into concrete and electromagnetics. Just all the cosmos together united part of the same trout bear wild rose star everyone has a part to play, and it's one big unfathomable miracle.

So, you ask, isn't everything on Earth part of this all-encompassing universe? Don't Crown Imperials and glowing mice and Aspen Maps have a part to play? They are, after all, made of natural materials, however scrambled those materials may be. No. Nature's definition of nature is that every being, living and nonliving, evolved and created, participates in the continuity of the whole. Imperialism's technologies, psychologies, and ideologies lunge like freeways toward the linear horizon, never knowing their place or purpose or end point, producing in their wake a disruption so massive it cannot be made sustainable.

It has been said that the attraction of empire's artifacts and assumptions is their glamour, their shine, the ease they afford the human effort. Perhaps most importantly, attraction springs from the reverberation of the archetypal within them, and herein we find the source of urgency displayed by the people who defend them. After all, virtual reality's invention *is* an exciting mental adventure, and exciting mental adventures have always stirred the human mind. Genetic engineering *does* speak to the urge within the psyche to participate in the unfolding of evolution, to seed fruits into the soil, to paint rock walls, to thin the herd, to shift identity and shape during ceremony. Princess Cruise! BMW! United Airlines! The truth is, humans have *always* traveled about the Earth. And the urban environmentalist who fights tooth and nail to keep native peoples off their native lands, while projecting his own sad split between human and nature, *is* in fact motivated by a passion to save trees and whales.

But the context is all wrong, is upside down and twisted all around, the dysfunctional and the archetypal becoming so interwoven as to be indistinguishable. In the imperial context, the earnest defense of virtual nature *feels* right. No, it does *not* feel right; it settles over the mind like a wind without the breeze. And pain of all pains, such confusion and contradiction reside at every turn, deviously convoluted, matted, enmeshed, nasty hair balls on the floor of empire.

("Mi gente." Oso rises up into the confusion. With dignity, as if he were adjusting a handwoven vest, he smooths down his Burger King T-shirt. We are being treated to the 100 AKER WOOD side of his personality. "Mi gente. We have tried many things, ¿qué no?"

A few heads nod within the pine walls of the cabin. A few bodies straighten up from their sad arch toward the shag rug. Just then a chorus of neighs echoes from outside and a few clops, as if the horses were also attempting to gather themselves into a new arrangement.

Tomás is back with his eyes. "Pasamos dutifully a la legislature every January. They still have their hold on us. If we want to make a change in how we do things, all of Nuevo México has to OK it. So every year we make the long viaje to the capital with our problems. We stand around in the halls like everyone, y we talk all day long. Last year we asked that we be able to elect our officers every two years instead of one, y we got it."

"This action es sólo para certain things, ¿qué no?" Mambo says. "Es para que we don't have el gobierno down our backs on a daily basis."

I have learned that Snowflake is a reflective man, even shy. Yet he is right in there with this talk. "It seems we are always fighting," he raises his voice from the back table. "Él que mantiene, tiene. Y él que no, ni derecho tiene."

"¿Do you remember that time La Floresta gave our mesa to a big corporation?" Here comes Oso's grizzly bear side. "¡ Just *gave* it away!" he snarls. "Y they were about to start the clear-cutting, cabrones. All the bulldozers y earthmovers were ready. ¡Y we shot up las máquinas con our .30-06s pa' la chingada!"

"¿How about when that big old bank started the ATM by the apple shed? Muelas y Antonio fueron pa'yá con sus hunting rifles y blasted that sucker into shreds. ¡*We* showed them how to take money out of the bank!"

A kick-ass wildness is erupting. "¡No vamos a olividar el gran ataque de sorpresa!" "¡Que viva!" someone shouts. "¡Tratamos a get back the land grant y we busted into the courthouse y we ourselves arrested the police!"

Kick-ass stops short. The event holds deep meaning and hard memories. It is reported to the rest of the nation on ABC News and in the *New York Times*. I remember. I am in Berkeley. The year is 1967, and the event is part of the whole international swirl of protest of the times — antiwar and the women's movement, the Trots and the Socialist Workers, liberation struggles in Algeria and Ireland and Nicaragua, the Black Panther Party. All of a sudden, from virtually no known location in the American psyche, emerge these rural Chicanos fighting for their lands by inventing their own authority. In the process, a New Mexico State Police officer is wounded, a UPI reporter and a sheriff's deputy taken hostage. After the fray, several of the activists are set up by the feds, drugs planted in their trucks in hopes of putting them away for a long, long time.

Oso stands up. He is soft again like an oatmeal bear. "Mi gente, no hay soluciones fáciles, ¿no?")

THE SAME PLACE

What's next? King Lear in Tahiti?

— Ann Lawrence Ryan, "Much Ado Sobre Nada"

We are all one. This is what the world's religions proclaim. The Earth is a single living organism. So declare the photographs taken on *Apollo 17*. And now here come the cries from the post-colonial cartographer. Carte blanche! Carte blanche! he exclaims. Let's make it *all* the same! Every person on Earth served up the same bag of fries, linked to the same cyberspace, fed the same techno-utopian fantasy. Every person — Violet, Snowflake, myself — forced into subsisting by the same political-economic rules.

And every location too. Cleveland. Helsinki. Mexico. Every place divided and subdivided into neat little checkerboards of private ownership. Every place at the fingertips of the transnational stock exchange. No more regional uniqueness. No more sovereignty. No more sustainability. Every place the same.

I peer over the steel railing on level 6 of the Denver International Airport. This is a big room. I mean *big*. It is the central atrium — at its peak 126 feet from floor to ceiling, walled at the south end entirely in glass and crested by the airport's dramatic signature, its caravan-style Teflon-coated roof. I feel lost.

The total size of the airport is fifty-three square miles. My God! After you make it through the entrance plaza, you have to proceed another two miles to the terminal. To flatten the site, bulldozers and earthmovers have hauled off 110 million cubic yards of high-desert soil. Two and a half million cubic yards of concrete have been hauled in to make the runways, taxiways, and aprons; more for the 18,000-car parking lot. The airport's 1,200 flight-information and baggage-claim display monitors are dependent on 5,300 miles of fiber-optic cable, a distance longer than the River Nile. There is a cactus garden and a native art collection — each representing something that has been obliterated to make the airport in the first place. And accomplishment of accomplishments, the Denver International Airport is set to accommodate a grand total of 88,000 passengers a day. Skiers. Tourists. Businesspeople. Students. Salesmen. Conference-goers. All stampeding to and from the ticket counters, through the security pavilions, up and down the escalators, on and off the subway trains. The promotional literature boasts that the airport can handle 2,000 pairs of skis in a single hour — and 48,000 skiers in a day.[1]

Why so big? Why so spectacular? In 1998, 500 million, or half a billion, of the world's 5.7 billion people took international journeys, and the United Nations' World Tourism Organization estimated that this would soon rise to 650 million — with five times as many traveling within their own countries.[2] That's a total of 3 billion tourists.[3]

I am not a skier or a tourist. Decades after Berkeley, I am still a political activist. I am returning home now from a speaking engagement on the social effects of the global economy. But I am a solitary wayfarer in this vast vacuum of a space. The question that riddles my mind is this: where are the 87,999 other passengers?

After witnessing two commercial airplanes slam into the World Trade Center towers and seeing the Pentagon and a field in Pennsylvania burn, many potential nomads have soured on air travel, opting now to drive, take a train, or stay home.

I see something I have never seen in an American airport: two young men on the far escalator wearing jungle fatigues and black lace-up boots. They are carrying submachine guns.

Just then I catch sight of two other young men, and they are walking directly toward me. These fellows are decidedly different from their contemporaries in uniform. Dressed REI from head to toe, they are shouldering a couple of towering backpacks with aluminum tent poles and ripstop tarps cascading over the top. The tall one has a blond bristle of a beard, and he is carrying a book, *When Corporations Rule the World,* by David Korten. Seeing it, I am jolted out of the social paralysis fostered by this steel mausoleum.

"Excuse me." I reach out and tap the young man's arm. "I noticed your book."

"Yeah!" He swivels toward me, the paraphernalia above his head pivoting like a skyscraper on a turntable. He is an enthusiastic sort. "Wow!" he oozes. "I didn't know this book. The title grabbed me."

"David Korten is a colleague of mine."

"Really? Too much," the other man pipes up. "It's mind-blowing, this global economy. We felt so strongly about it we protested in Seattle in 1999 and again in Genoa in 2001. We're just back now from Malaysia where we got to see the last of the rain forest."

"What are these places like?" I ask.

"They're all the same, " says the blond. "Everybody eats at McDonald's and drinks Coke. And now everybody everywhere is scared. No one is traveling. I mean the airports are *just* like this."

"Like a TV screen humming with nothing on it," adds the other man.

We are standing by the down escalator. A half a football field away a lone passenger clutching a nylon dress bag appears beside a kiosk like an alien. Suddenly self-consciousness grips us: for God's sake, people don't *talk* to each other in places like this!

"Uh . . ." stutters the blond man. I sense our brief moment is coming to a close.

"Well," I offer, opening my arm like a magician to highlight the mega-atrium surrounding us. "This is it: *when corporations rule the world.*"

With no forewarning, as if in slow motion, everything on the surface of awareness seems to dissolve. Our eyes are unexpectedly peeled of preconception, and for one long moment we gaze together at this vast human-constructed space, glass and steel, Teflon and copper, submachine guns and military helmets, electromagnetic fields penetrating to our bones, and signs everywhere LUFTHANSA MEXICANA TWA everywhere shrieking CONTINENTAL DELTA UNITED.

"Yeah, this is *it*." In a wink, the two men disappear down the escalator.

To the former colonies, "it" has meant a stampede of international airports and Club Meds and endless buses of tourists seeking respite in paradise. Third World religious leaders met in Manila in 1980 to discuss the impact of "it" on local cultures. Their conclusion was startling. Within the empire, travel to any locale on the planet is, after all, viewed as an inalienable right. They made a challenge: "Tourism does more harm than good to people and to societies of the Third World," they countered. Dr. Koson Srisang, a leader of the Ecumenical Coalition of Third World Tourism that resulted from the meeting, said that tourism as currently practiced "does not benefit the majority of people. Instead it exploits them, pollutes the environment, destroys the ecosystem, bastardises the culture, robs people of their traditional values and ways of life and subjugates women and children in the abject slavery of prostitution. . . . [It] epitomizes the present unjust world economic order where the few who control wealth and power dictate the terms."[4]

OK. Here's a better plan. It's not a unique plan. In fact, in some circles, you'd have to admit it is ordinary. Expected. Assumed. Desired. Or maybe it isn't a plan at all. Maybe, in the wake of classical empire, people are forced by the exigencies of immediate survival to imagine such things. Maybe this is just how things are unfolding. Or could it be the will of the deities?

Whatever, it's happening . . .

Oh Lord. There was a book called *It's Happening*. I read it in 1967. It was about the explosion of political awareness and cultural experimentation that took place in the 1960s. I know there were plenty of people who were not pleased by the times, who were outright terrified. But I was thrilled. It was my life, and it laid the ground for all future meaning.

Now I am the one to be displeased. It's happening. Take Malaysia. Gaining its independence from Great Britain after World

War II, this "undeveloped" nation stepped into thorny terrain. It had been mowed over in every way, from the psychological to the economic, and it was now attempting to unfurl its flag into a world busily restructuring into a subtler form of the same old bag.

Take Vision 2020. Now *here's* a plan. A plan to transform Malaysia, with its paradisiacal rain forests and rice paddies and rubber trees, into the planet's most seductive technobusiness park. The Multimedia Super Corridor would link the immense new Kuala Lumpur International Airport with two newly constructed cities — a digital-friendly capital called Putrajaya and an infotech center named Cyberjaya — all knit together by fiber optics and managed by a WTO-ready code of cyber-laws. Good-bye rubber tappers, basket weavers, and thatched villages. Hello CEOs, Banana Republic–clad infoworkers, and one-bedroom condominiums. The land would be coated in concrete. Superfreeways would glide into the horizon like boulevards at Versailles. There would be corporate headquarters galore, computer-smart campuses, borderless marketing plexes, and national cyber-cards to access everything from one's IQ to overdue video-rental fines. What cattle are left would inhabit patches of pasture the size of one-bedroom condos and graze on plastic shopping bags.

Vision 2020. It's being thrust down the throat of reality by Malaysia's prime minister, Dr. Mahathir bin Mohamad, who has already distinguished himself by supplanting the rubber trees of the north to build a modern multiversity, erecting the world's two tallest spires, building superhighways where only footpaths existed before, jamming them with the indigenous-built Proton, and jacking up the gross national product from $34 billion in 1980 to $123 billion in 1995.[5]

It's happening.

To attempt such contrivances — no matter by assassination, corporate buyout, or TV ad — requires a certain state of mind. This is a psychology begotten by a way of life that is fundamentally unmanageable and unsustainable. Its bedrock is the opposite of solid: chronic uncertainty, and chronic uncertainty begets anxiety. Then, to mask the attendant afflictions — the nightmares and the terror — there is denial.

Not surprisingly, native peoples are the ones to pose the pertinent question, reversing the reversal: *who is the savage?* they ask. And indeed, when history unveiled its tragic plot, when the European mapmaker came upon native peoples in their furs and feathers, a rude challenge flew in his face. Who *are* these people? it urged. Or more precisely, who am *I?* With only anxiety and denial as resources for answers, the imperial mind became desperate. Immediate relief was demanded — and achieved in the enactment (sometimes explosive, sometimes meticulous) of dominance, narcissism, and violence.

That damn snowball. It just keeps right on rolling. Down down through fear, bouncing into terror, picking up bulk as it goes, picking up speed, smashing everything in its wake. Who's to hold on? And *how?* Direct control through military offense connects with control by the dollar. Formerly self-sustaining peoples are denied their land, coerced and seduced into dependence on Exxon and Wal-Mart, left holding the same bag of fries as everyone else. "Us" and "other." Other. Other. And within the imperial mind, if there is any mind left, terror recedes like melting snow. Fascination picks up speed. Helplessly surrounded by freeways, native and land-based peoples become less the savage threat of yesteryear, more the backdrop for unnamed longings, fantasies, projections — and corporate exploitation of such vulnerabilities. "WASH CIVILIZATION OFF YOU!" teases the Isuzu ad.[6] Spend your vacation in paradise! Make love in a tepee! Drive a sport utility vehicle down Park Avenue! Study with a shaman!

And meanwhile, everything that was once coherent is impossibly scrambled. Be alert: this is not the intermingling of cultural artifact and assumption that has always sustained humanity. Here the DNA of peoples' ways and beliefs is hacked cavalierly from its sources, implanted erratically into foreign terrain. What is produced is a jumble of cultural and not-so-cultural fragments, African drums and Nike shoes, vision quests and Yugo sedans and Blue Willow tea sets all mixed up, all enmeshed world-music cruise-to-heaven — courtesy of the World Trade Organization.

It is no wonder that those within the jumble are looking so desperately for archetypes.

("No hay soluciones fáciles." Viola is pacing around the inner arc of the circle. It is getting to be late afternoon. The sun is pouring through the one window, channeling a square of brilliance onto the orange rug. "Ahora things are heating up."

"How you say it is how it is," says Mambo. "There seems to be a plan, ¿qué no? pero we don't get to know nothing about it."

A skinny man with a Snap-On Tool cap and jeans draping from his hipbones waves one finger into the air. "I work for the highway department," he announces.

Of course everyone already knows this. Everyone but me. His consideration of my presence in the midst of intense discussion is remarkable. Snowflake echoes the consideration.

"This man es mi primo," he whispers. "Snap-On Gonzales."

Snap-On is insistent. "It is worse than a bullfight," he calls out. "They are building a six-lane freeway from Socorro to Espa. Cloverleafs, airports, todo." With the exception of the tonnages of concrete we call Albuquerque and Santa Fe, the stretch of road from Socorro to Española cuts through nothing but tumbleweed terrain for 150 miles. "They are making a mega-superhighway for mega-super-companies."

"¿Computadores?" wonders Oso.

"Sí. Como un lugar llamado Silicon Valley."

Tomás paces nervously alongside Viola, his left hand blanketing a mouth that, were it visible, would surely reveal shock. His worn boots halt in the square of sunlight.

"There is another plan," he says. "About water. They are saying la adquisición del agua, its value, will be figured on how much money it makes."

"Pero las acequias don't make money," marvels Snowflake. "They make corn y chile y hay for the horses."

"Cae en la cuenta, mi amigo, you get the point. According to this new water plan, our way of life does not have a bank account."

"¡Y real estate!" José interjects. "They are selling the Vigil place, pero they don't even tell us in the village. They don't put up any sign, y some ricos from Hollywood are buying it por completo."

"Por más dinero que podemos imaginar. The Vigil land went for half a million American dollars."

"¿Y quiénes son nuestros vecinos? Con sus puertas eléctricas y especialmente porque viven en Califas, our neighbors are nobody."

"¡Híjole!" Viola is more upset than we have seen her. "Mis niños, all they want is Nike shoes like the people from Hollywood. ¡Dinero, dinero, puro dinero! Lo que no tenemos."

This time it is I who am feeling like revving up and taking off like a rocket. I cup my message into Snowflake's ear. "May I say something?"

"¡Por supuesto! You talked before."

"But they *asked* me to talk."

"We want to hear you talk. You know things different than we do." He waves his hand in the air and points down at me.

Once again, I find myself sitting at the center of a respectful silence.

"Thank you, Snowflake, Tomás, Viola, Oso, everyone. . . . I . . . ah . . . have something to say. . . . I want you to know that what you are describing is not just happening to you. It is happening everywhere. . . . You know all about the conquest of the last five hundred years. This is a new conquest. And for all the ways it sucks you in, for all the new trucks and running shoes, the world the TV dangles before you is the new imperialism." I am struggling. I want to speak in a way they can take in. "This new way of life, it's not about you making decisions for your families and villages and land. It's about banks and companies and politicians making all the plans. I live in the valley. Everybody sits around and talks about how things used to be. With this new imperialism, no one will even remember how it used to be."

"¡Híjole, I can't even remember where I put my horse!" cackles old José, and a welcome lightness flies through the cabin like a butterfly.

"¡Y tu caballo no quiere recordar a donde estas tú!" Rosalía pokes at José, and everyone laughs.

"Nobody will want to remember," I say. "There'll be more companies like Duke City and Summo coming in to clear-cut and mine. There'll be more busloads of German tourists and more Hollywood neighbors. More fights over different ways of thinking, like this battle with the environmentalists. More nuclear weapons up at Los Alamos. Did you think that the lab would slow down because the Cold War is over? No way! Now they have to build weapons to protect the corporations! There'll be more biotech research too. And anti-terrorism work. And you watch: there'll be less growing chile. Less hunting. Less fishing. Less water for irrigation. There'll be more Long John Silver and Taco Bell. It'll be just like everywhere else. This new imperialism is hell-bent on making every place exactly like every other place."

"I have a friend from Laguna Pueblo who told me a vision," the man in the red bandana says. "He was over there on 285, y all of a sudden his mind opens up, he sees that place. ¡It looks like Burbank, Califas! Freeways. Cloverleafs. Smog. Big old buildings everywhere."

Tomás' black eyes laser into mine. "¿How did this happen?"

"Well," I make a stab. "After World War II, colonized people everywhere rebelled. And there were liberation movements inside the imperial nations, you know better than me, civil rights, la raza. The bankers and government leaders and companies got nervous, so they passed laws to let big corporations go into foreign places and get whatever they want without having to own the country. Gold. Lumber. Water. Workers. They took away local control and made everyone dependent on their money. You talk about the Sacred Word. According to the new Sacred Word, you don't have rights anymore. You can pass a law in New Mexico to protect the forest or stop toxic dumping. But if a company in Switzerland says your law gets in the way of its profit, the law gets thrown out."

Tomás is dead still. "They are telling us this is democracy . . .")

The pain travels everywhere. You step through the threshold of the airport metal detector. Against all odds the pain slips through, follows you along the walking-escalator, taps you on the shoulder, grips your heart. Rochester. Forest. Delphos. DELTA. UNITED. Los montes. Las casas. Terrorist hideouts and techno-business parks. Nothing of this whole Earth is unknown, inside and out, everywhere is the same. Everywhere there is pain.

One entanglement of pain and memory wraps its tentacles around the one before, ensnaring me without warning or respite. The only time I am left in calm is when I work: my psyche gives me this little gift. The rest of the time I am knotted in the threadbare noose of imperialism's making. The syringe. The sanitarium. My brother's frozen horror. Motels. My mother's white-linen world, irrelevant in its inability to see or admit. I am exhausted by grief, incapacitated by fear. My hair falls out. My nerves shriek roseolas everywhere on my scalp, on the insides of my thighs, up my back. I get migraines. When events press in from the here and now, my psyche wraps itself around them, seeking out any parallel to the past, any thread that is reminiscent. My twenty-year-old Scout breaks down: I am flooded with memories of rapes in Packards and Buicks. A trip to an indigenous peoples' antinuclear hearing in Europe becomes the forum for my fear of motel rooms. An alcoholic prancing like a crazed rooster threatens to kill me, and I stand face-to-face with the challenge of defending myself. The healing goes on and on and on, unbearably on, because the abuse went on and on and on. Pimples are bursting everywhere, pustules erupting from deep festering, boils oozing their dreaded tales.

A relationship to the oozing develops. Feelings, memories, and physical symptoms have previously been fractured from one another. As they erupt now into full awareness, my task is to bear them. Even welcome them. Yes. I am the hurt child, the desperate child, the hopeless teenager, the sick adult. But I am also the nurse, mopping up the pus, bandaging the lesions, and soothing, always soothing. Who I am in the deepest sense is something bigger than these feelings, these memories, these symptoms. Who I am is shaped by the sky and the rain and the buckeye. Political prisoners who resist empire's thrust become mythic to me. Jail, beatings, torture — and yet some of them are able to maintain their connection to the goodness of Creation. Some, miraculously, emerge to become leaders and visionaries.

Healing. It is such a big job. It is the most important job in my life. Few people know or understand. They think of me as an external persona: a writer, a psychotherapist, a political activist, a jokester with a raucous laugh. When they discover what lies at the core of my existence, some are disturbed and flee. Others self-righteously insist I am wrong. Still others tell me they are sorry; I didn't have it so bad, they quiver. Amid such antics of discomfort, the question becomes: am I an oddity? An aberration? No. I am just another in this world of earthly whereabouts Bengal Mexico Cleveland making my way through the pain that is empire.

Like everyone else, I have no map.

OFF THE MAP

You thought
America
was on a map

— Demetria Martinez, "Discovering America"

THE BORDER

When borders gain a paradoxical centrality, margins, edges, and lines of communication emerge as complex maps and histories.

— James Clifford, *Routes*

The borders are marked by distinct, preferably straight lines. On the map they are black or red-brown lines. In reality they are six-foot cyclone fences. Swirls of barbed wire. Checkpoints swarming with federal mosquitoes, high-intensity floodlights. And yet anyone who lives at the perimeter — between empire's insistence and its negation, between trauma and denial — knows that the border is a territory of greater magnitude and dimension than a line or a fence.

So many borders, so little understanding of terrain. This is how it is for us. The map breaks down. Its certainty fades like the symbols at the creased edge of a TripTik that has been folded into oblivion. Like the false-hue colors on a screen whose hard drive is just now crashing. On the edge. Brink. Fringe.

On the verge.

We turn to the geography of reality. It is fraught with the paradoxes and contradictions cast by generations and generations of empire. We turn to the cartography of truth. It is twisted, distorted on the insistence of those who, clinking crystal and ice cubes, seek vindication in their own versions of things.

They are saying that the architectural plans for Auschwitz reveal no rooms suitable for gas chambers, that the Holocaust therefore did not take place. They are saying that the natives after all sacrificed human flesh to the gods, that they deserved to be mastered. They are saying that the people are part conqueror, that they themselves stole the land, that therefore the United States government should keep it. They are saying so many things. That Chevron Oil cares for butterflies. That the children made up the stories. They are saying that we will require distinct boundaries, chain-link and barbed-wire, to delineate what is and what is not.

The truth. What really happened? Who did what? Where? When? To whom? Who was there to witness? Which story will in the end be told? Some of the stories come terminally entangled with rage and shame and grief. Others appear clean. What stories, in the most private moments of our minds, do we ourselves admit? Could it be possible that there is simply too much pain? Could it be that the twisting tracks to the incapacity of the psyche to handle the complexity of pressures caused by so much agony?

(The woman standing next to me brushes her fingers lightly against my hair. Then she cries across the cabin. "¡Estoy cansada de llorar!" "Sí," interjects Viola. "Estamos tired of crying.")

In the coach. At the checkpoint. YOU ARE HERE: in the front seat or the back; by heritage, by choice, by circumstance, by necessity. If this border is like any other, it is probable that those of us who hail from the dominant society will get through. The man with the mustache and epaulets approaches stiffly, leans into the driver's-side window to look us over. Acting normal, we hand him our papers. Everything appears to be in order. He waves us on. It is not so likely that Snowflake will make it. The guard uses a stern voice to order him out of the car. Blood stampedes through his organs. German shepherds lick the upholstery of the car; his legs are searched.

But this border that I am talking about is off the map. This is the uncharted territory that lies between empire and colonization. At this checkpoint, it is you and I who are going to be searched.

The exigencies that we have long overlooked become immediately clear. Oh God! We *want* to get through! Can we survey the terrain so we can make our way without being noticed? Whip out our astrolabes and multispectral scanners? Go linear? Can we bring our Jones Live-Map Meters? Sprinkle green sugar to indicate the forests, silver balls for the capitals?

I have it from Snowflake that we cannot. A model crafted of something more earthbound, maybe willow sticks and corn husks, he proposes, strapped together to display the lay of the land. Add desert pebbles to pinpoint the exact locations of strength and meaning. Imagine: you could collect the materials behind the house, he says. You could twist and bind them to make a map. Then, like the ancient cartographers of the South Pacific, you would memorize your creation. And when at last you launch, you would leave it behind; you would put your bodies against the wind and feel the way with your bones.

How to construct a stick/corn/pebble map. We begin with discomfort. It is a discomfort born of having our heads shot through with messy bullet holes in the seventh grade, enhanced by decades of watching television. We do not know the truth. But when the truth is finally revealed, when the voices of the colonized penetrate to our hearts, the discomfort does not subside. It grows. We are transported to a world so fraught with contradiction it is as if we are being pierced by a medieval sword trap.

We are hardly alone. The hallmark of the native experience is the juxtaposition of conflicting worlds. Two languages. Two ways of thinking. Two stories of origin. Two feelings for land. Two legal systems. Two notions of what is human. At the 1993 International Testimonials on the Violation of Indigenous Sovereignty Rights, two political strategy workshops go on at once: one on hard organizing to gain support for sovereignty struggles within the United Nations; the other, equally serious, on creating a kind of parallel-universe indigenous-based United Nations that, no matter the successes or failures of the first effort, gives legitimacy to a reality that is believed but not embodied.

Two worlds. The empire and the conquered. And you and I, here within the empire, after centuries and generations of the certainty of our maps: it is our time to reside at the border between worlds that do not mesh.

I have done the work of remembrance, catharsis, and understanding. I am confident there are no more untoward events still hidden in my psyche. And I have reaped the benefits of my efforts: capacities that stood before as unattainable goals are now mine. I have not been sick for over a decade. And I am no longer afraid to speak. I can get a decent night's sleep in a motel room. The migraines and hives have disappeared. My best offering to life, my creativity, is blossoming as I could not have imagined. And miracle of miracles, I have made a home, having purchased a house in a village in northern New Mexico. Most important, I have strength inside. And equanimity. Life unfolds as a quiet celebration.

But I am not finished. I seem to be residing within a borderland that is not a place of trauma and stress — but not yet a place of healing. Some serious symptoms hang on, and there is a feeling like a rocky shoreline. One night, in the gauzy dreamworld, I find myself surrounded by racks and racks of corporate laptop wear, skirts and blouses and jackets all made in sweatshops in Indonesia, all exactly the same. I am ambling awkwardly among the garments, a freak wrapped from head to toe in medical bandages: unacceptable, not yet revealed. This last stretch of the journey is as trying as was the beginning. I have accomplished the bulk of the inner work, and yet I am still grappling to *believe*. After a lifetime of knowing only the psychic fragmentation that has protected me from the truth, to become true to myself lies within vision — and yet seems beyond reach.

Complex maps and histories: the very stuff that stick/corn/stone maps are made to chart. Every day you and I are stymied by the contradictions fabricated in our world. There is the problem of things. The newspaper on the chair. Bringing news of massacres and toxic spills. Itself made of 150-year-old Engelmann spruce and Cariboo fir from British Columbia. Cooked into pulp in a stew of sodium sulfide. Bleached with chlorine dioxides that exhale deadly dioxins. Printed with petroleum-based resins from California, carbon-black from oil drilled in the Gulf of Mexico, colored inks produced in the industrial suburbs of Seattle. Delivered in a van fueled by gasoline from Saudi Arabia. Bound by a petroleum-based rubber band made in Hong Kong. Sheathed in a polyethylene bag from New Jersey.[1] The newspaper. Bringing news of suffering, itself causing suffering.

This white linen shirt. Constructed in a sweatshop in Indonesia. Or Lithuania. Or Saipan. Everything of this world. Shoes made of Brazilian cattle whose grazing lands were once rain forest. Eggs on the plate: they come courtesy of hens buckling in boxes not twice the size of their bodies, shot up with antibiotics and hormones. These petrochemical lawn chairs. Earl Grey tea. Everything. The raw materials of our lives mean one thing as we obtain them glistening at the mall, via the Internet, in mail-order catalogs, as gifts from friends. They mean something else in the naked sober world of their origin. They are literally made of the oppression, pain, grief, sacrifice imposed by the global economy.

Then there is the problem of work. Oh Lord. Already we are having a hard time with work. Already we are attempting against all odds to provide for our families and enact values through our livelihoods. And yet whatever money we earn and how we use it to survive in the workaday world only maintain the hegemony of the system that — by nature of its takeover of land, removal of people, and forced dependence on corporate livelihood — destroys families and robs us of values. Then in an effort to be upstanding citizens, or maybe just to stay out of trouble, we pay taxes. The taxes buy more than medical care for welfare mothers and streetlights; they subsidize multinationals like Lockheed Martin; they produce weapons of mass destruction whose post–Cold War purpose is to shield corporations from insurrection. Yes, we are paid-up citizens. But we are not feeling very upstanding, and we are most certainly not staying out of trouble.

We are challenged to do something. Yet how do we choose what to do when the options themselves clash like armies of fire ants? Do we work to alleviate poverty by corraling people made destitute into the system that made them poor in the first place? Do we support the construction of massive, unsustainable infrastructures for predicaments whose roots lie in the decimation of sustainable infrastructures? Salve public health epidemcs caused by increasing exposure to toxic substances with doctoring that relies on toxic substances?

Confusion awaits us at every turn. What about this war against terrorism? To fight terrorism is righteous from the standpoint of defense: Americans do not want to endure any more violence against innocent citizens. But the act of fighting terrorism produces untenable contradiction. The pursuit of fuel to run the war cancels all concern for the health of the Earth. Civil liberties are dismantled so that potential infiltrators may be routed out. Land-based peoples fighting for their cultures and homelands are suddenly labeled terrorists. In fact, *anyone* challenging the triumph of the corporate marketplace becomes a terrorist, while globalization is billed as a "right" alongside political representation and trial by jury. Besides, haven't we seen this intense projection of "evil" and "God's will" at other times in history — and with disastrous results? And didn't someone say that violence begets violence which begets more violence?

Indeed, we are grappling to stay afloat in a sea of contradictions. When we try to get a grip on a life-preserver, things only become more slippery. Conflict among the people working to make a better world is sprouting like Starbucks coffee shops. Take a look: some activists seek a future of planetary oneness based on high-tech communications; others insist the new technologies are sinister extensions of corporate control. Feminists: they are busy arguing about the definition of female nature. Some activists end up creating the same competitive hierarchies in their organizations that they are confronting in the world. And the environmentalists: indeed, they are working to protect the very lifeblood of our future survival — what few natural places are left — but in the urgency of the crisis, they too often make refugees of the land-based peoples whose cultural knowledge offers. . . the very lifeblood of our future survival.

Everything is topsy-turvy. Yes, we are fighting for social justice, cultural beauty, community togetherness, and environmental preservation. But to do so, we add to toxic dissemination and ozone depletion by driving cars and taking airplanes. We stay home with our computers. Again. The problem of things. The infohighway magnifies toxicity by its manufacture, causes immunological diseases among workers, exposes users to electromagnetic radiation, is fueled by electricity garnered from dams and nuclear power. OK. So all torn up inside, or numb, we travel to escape the clutch of consumerism and contradiction. We move around, blow town. We bring consumerism and contradiction with us wherever we go.

Complex maps and histories. How could such untenable juxtapositions come to be? Twist corn husk. Lash willow sticks together. The truth of land and time and peoples is revealed. Nothing is as simple or pure as it appeared in the seventh grade. We are mapping the historical mixing of empires. Of Chinese with Japanese. French and British. Spanish with Moor. We are tending to the tentacles of our own empire. This task alone is enough to occupy us forever, and yet the empire that is charted over North America is itself stitched with threads of Arabian star nights and Roman law and Aztec vegetables. We are mapping the mixing — and we are mapping the gobbling of empires by other empires. Rome swallowing Greece; the Middle East, North Africa; Great Britain, the Middle East. And there is more: maps not of colonizations at the edge, but of colonizations within the empire itself. Of conquered natives. Of children abused. Of the militarization of men. And workers whose designated purpose is none other than to build wealth for the wealthy. Then there is the inevitable interweaving of empire with colonized. Servant children born to rapist masters. Settlers in solidarity with natives. Love across class. Nouveau imperialists within tribes. The newly colonized.

Look here. I have found a long willow branch, fine and rich in its redness, curved at the end like an old staff. This willow remembers the ancient question, the one that lies behind the irreconcilable juxtapositions we are charting. *Whose land is this anyway?* it begs. *Whose trees? Whose water? Whose air?* Whether our people were zealous conquerors of the seventeenth century or well-meaning settlers, whether they fled to Ellis Island from eastern Europe in 1905 or arrived last week, the system we participate in and depend on ripped into this continent in a deliberate act of takeover. It assumes its place and performs its affairs today on stolen lands.

My land is stolen. "MK and CC, for consideration paid, grant to Chellis Glendinning the following described real estate in New Mexico." The exchange seems simple enough: I own .42 acre and a house. But the deed goes on: *"Subject to restrictions, reservations, and/or easements of record."* Ah! Here's the catch! The actual restrictions on the plot I call mine are in fact far more complex than can be documented in the county records. Originally the land was free and open, here by the cool of the river, used as a summer place by the natives scattered east from Chaco Canyon. Then, with the arrival of people up from Mexico, it became parcel to the commons of the land grant and was given protection under the Treaty of Guadalupe Hidalgo. How is it that this land came up for sale and I bought it?

Snowflake is feeling cantankerous. "This land is not good for nothing except putting a house," he quips, meaning it is not farmland or pasture or hunting grounds. And yet to me, coming from the city, it is paradise. Pink earth. Grasses. Piñon. Juniper. The acequia streams beneath the cottonwood at the west end. And here: the house, pine logs and mud bricks, in perfect position to behold the ledges of the barrancas to the south.

But look, gazing out the window by my desk, a corrugated metal sign looms across the fence: NO TRESSPASSING, it scowls in spray paint, GET OUT. The sign is not entirely distinct from the handmade marker at Piglet's house in 100 AKER WOOD: TRESPASSERS W, this one announces — except that unlike the usual signs in Pooh's and Piglet's world, TRESPASSERS W is Webster-spelled. The billboard facing my window is not NO TRESSPASSING, it revs its high-rider engine. *Whose land?* it presses.

How to construct a stick/corn map. The question becomes: who are we, you and I? Colonized or empire? Oppressed or perpetrator? Manipulated, duped, or fully aware? Am I Irish or English? Are you Russian or Jew?

I have been hanging with a group of Navajo uranium miners in Gallup. It has been a dusty journey in an old Chevy pickup truck from Shiprock, over to Chinle and Canyon de Chelly, down to Fort

Defiance and into the trading-post city. We are sitting at last around a red Naugahyde booth, expectant of scrambled eggs and pancakes and burgers, and the conversation ambles its way along the border where the native world juxtaposes the colonizer. My friend Chester announces, "You are of the dominant society." I am stunned. I fled my ancestors' house so long ago. I have spent a lifetime outside it, done all I can to reveal its excesses. I do not think of myself as being *of* it. But there it is. I creep around the idea, poke at it, try it on. Sure enough, I am of the dominant society.

Complex borders, untoward currents. Where are we? How to navigate? Whether riding in the front seat or the back, we too are twisted and hurt by the system that aims to rule the world; we are the wounded shuffling among the racks of corporate suits. And yet, knowing the unspeakable agonies imposed upon colonized peoples, where is the place for expression of *our* pain? *Our* power? Such query remains unsolved. Behind it, the original question haunts still like gaggles of wild ghosts and skeletons falsetto howling: *whose land? whose trees? whose water?* Their unrelenting insistence on the truth always, always in the backdrop of our lives highjacks all expression. Our fear: we are unacceptable. In the face of such unresolved contradiction: we are not yet revealed.

How to construct a stick/corn/stone map. Gather willow. The borderlands we are charting make no sense at all. And look: the colonized are crossing without us, creating maps we cannot even decipher. Twist husks. Weave them into patterns. Hold everything you find close to your heart.

("Comadres, compadres, we know it in our hearts." Tomás stands tall. "Es la hora, it is time." The remembering, the detailing of the problems, the questioning, the pacing: his dedication congeals into a single resolve. "Tenemos que caminar de un lado al otro."

"We are doing what we can to keep la cultura." Viola appears to be thinking out loud. "It is time for us that we go ojo-a-ojo with the authorities of the Treaty of Guadalupe Hidalgo."

This is not a new thought in the history of native relations with the United States government. In New Mexico the people attempted open negotiation through the eras of the surveyor general and the Court of Public Land Claims; again in the 1950s when Congressman Joseph Montoya initiated legislation to review the situation; and again when Representative Bill Richardson promised to do the same. Nothing came of the efforts. But today the prospect is spoken with new confidence: for the first time it is spoken by people who know English well enough to distinguish a Sacred Word from a lie.

"We will pick cuatro embajadores," announces Tomás. "Four people to ride to the capital to meet with the keepers of the treaty. Four people to speak."

"Four wishes," Rosalía's voice crackles.

"Four demands," says the man in the bandana.

"Four directions," adds Oso.

"We will tell them in our own words. Es la hora pa' right the injustices."

"Somos indios," whispers Delfina. I think Snowflake and I may be the only ones to hear the utterance. She speaks louder: "Let us make our way together as we know how. We are working with the Forest Service well now, mejor que antes, pero let me say the truth: La Floresta no más."

"No más," interjects Mambo.

"Let us choose our embajadores."

The atmosphere instantly shifts as if the group were rolling up its collective shirtsleeve. Chairs are picked up and plunked down closer together. The process that unfolds is surprisingly effective and quick. Certainly there is ambition in the air, even competitiveness, and yet the overarching feel is one of regard for each other and respect for the outcome.

"Tomás must go," someone says.

Tomás nods his head. "I will go."

"¿Y Oso?"

Oso is immediate in his grasp of the task at hand. "It is a three-day ride," he says. "My back is still injured. Besides, I will be needed here if Tomás is gone."

Delfina stands up.

"I am young," she says. "My father's horse is strong. I speak well. I would like to be chosen." If there is a problem with the idea of a woman riding to the capital and acting as ambassador for the Frijoles Land Grant, it passes like a summer breeze rippling over the river.

"¡Sí!" someone calls out. "Delfina Montoya will ride."

Rosalía clears her throat. It is late in the afternoon now, and she does not attempt to stand up this time. "M'ijito rides like a bandido." Straw cowboy hats bob in agreement.

"OK." Tomás wraps up the decision. "Mambo it is."

There is one more saddle to fill. The cabin falls into a self-conscious hush. For the second time today, we can hear the wind blowing through a nearby canyon.

"It is right for us to be four." Tomás looks expectantly at the circle. From the fireplace ledge, Viola shifts her weight from one hip to the other. Someone coughs. The needles outside shimmy in the wind. A horse clops a loose shoe. José leans haltingly down past his knees, drags up his wooden cane from the floor, and props it under his arm.

"Pues," he begins. "Necesitamos un guía, a guide. Someone who knows the trails, where are the fences, when to fish and pick berries. I know the land perfectamente, pero tengo demasiados años, I am not young. There is only one person in this group who knows the land come yo."

"Dínos quien."

"Snowflake Martinez."

I feel a sudden twitch reverberate from Snowflake's joints through the backbone of the table and into my gut. He looks intently at the very serious and very careful consideration that is now gripping the group.

"Sí," someone muses at this fresh-cut thought. "Snowflake Martinez."

Tomás stares straight into Snowflake's eyes. For one instant I am feeling the seemingly unshakable union he and I have crafted on our ride. It loosens a tad. Snowflake slowly begins to nod his head up and down. It breaks.

"Sí," he answers. "I am afraid, órale, pero I will ride. I will ride from our world into the world de los norteamericanos. We have three nights before the full moon. We must leave now."

Suddenly I am afraid too.)

The border. (Truth and contradiction.) Look. Desert willow bends so easily. Shape it to reflect the currents of our lives and times. Strap corn husks like bandages around the points of connection. The map echoes the scale required: it is tangible; it is of the natural world. The map reveals the space: it is changing. What resides in the background is now bursting forward. (What is central) falls back. (Lies))) recede. Things merge reconstitute coincide.

HOME

Thus History begins once again.

— Pablo Neruda, "Written in the Year 2000"

A sudden flurry of Levi shirts and cowboy boots erupts. People are pushing wooden chairs to the wall, stacking the ones that will stack. Outside, the women are pulling elk jerky and tortillas and Tupperware containers filled with beans out of their saddlebags, wrapping them in shawls, handing them to Tomás, Delfina, Mambo, and Snowflake. Our ambassadors are checking their horses' girths, buckling their chaps, accepting extra fishing gear and bullets from the men. It is a summer near-sundown flurry.

I untie my pinto's reins and move her, complete with burgeoning bouquets of cota, to the edge. Finally they are ready. It seems. No. I can't tell. But Snowflake makes his way over to me.

"¿Are you OK?"

"Yes," I say. "Uh . . . I'm scared. No one else is riding to the valley. I'm not sure how to get home."

"You've got three hours of sunlight. Then the moon."

"Yeah." I stare down at my boots. Minuscule pebbles of sand clot the seams. "I am glad for you, Snowflake. To make this trip. It is right."

"Che." He lifts my chin so we are eye-to-eye. "I know you can make it. You know the monte now too." He smiles. "Y tienes huevos."

"It's OK," I say. "Your journey is more important."

"Che." He is staring right into my spirit. "Your journey is important too."

169

The flurry swirls around us mullein colors cracked leather blanket rolls and the constant chattering in Spanish. I am happy. Good luck Mambo this is historic handshakes and hugs. I am terrified. I don't have a map follow the sky no straight lines check every move against the point of sunset.

And suddenly I am alone in the saddle. I look down past the wooden round of my stirrup and, in the stark clarity that is called fear, I glimpse a pile of fresh coyote scat on the ground. It looks like a wad of pomegranate seeds meshed with sun-dried tomato mush. I spur my pinto. She breaks into a trot, and off I go, as always doing what in my village causes unceasing hilarity: English posting in a Western saddle.

However displaced we may be along the routes and roads of empire, the first order in the business of homecoming is relationship with the colonized. Did I warn you that this was going to take a bigness of spirit? A maturity of psyche? An ability to hold unsolved issues like grizzly bears within the soul? And here we are: all wrapped up in our medical bandages, infused with airport atriums and religious icons from other places, microchips in our socks and paradoxes beyond our abilities to solve, feeling put-upon amid more liars and perpetrators than we can count, whittled down into dreamers and fighters for mere fragments of a vision. Yes. It is we, you and I, who are called to relationship that will require coexistence with personal and historical conflict. The prospect shatters self-identity. It is enough to cause us to tremble, flee, grasp onto stiff ideologies, become liars and perpetrators ourselves. And damn it! We've already made an effort! We've already constructed maps that reflect the currents of our histories and our confusions . . . and soon we will have to . . . oh God . . . *go on without them.*

Humility.

Freedom from pride and arrogance. The experience embodies the exact opposite of what imperialism is about. *Humility.* The word itself spreads calm. It is not time to spout off all you know about the Mercator map on the classroom wall or a satellite's picture of the whole planet or all of sociology history economics psychology

religion. Pick up a handful of small stones. It is time to listen. Listen
to the shift of the wind through the needles, the call of water play-
ing on rock, the bursting of star into night. Listen to the voice of
the Yoruba the Toltec Tewa Mapuche Okanagan the Apache Vato
Sami the bro from the hood. The words. The feeling. The meaning.
Listen until you can speak what you hear as if it were your own. . . .
But you're a woman? you protest. You are Jewish? Irish? You've been
beaten? Sent to war? You exist now in the jaws of globalization? Yes.
There will be a place for your story. I am whispering: *just not now.*
Humility. Five hundred years. Two thousand. More. The relationship we seek will not blossom until you yourself are blossoming with
the struggles and insights of the colonized. You have been held at
gunpoint by the empire too? Stones and pebbles. The fact gives you
more depth for this task of understanding.

As the child of violence, I am humbled before the miracle that allows
for healing and tracks the intricate map leading in its direction. There
is no single moment when I arrive at the destination. Rather I creep
up on it from a myriad of trails. My awareness drops from the dizzi-
ness of dissociation back to the earth and into the bones and blood
of this life. I find myself in the here and now, making choices about
my place in the world, contemplating events and people in the context of life and death, values and meaning. I am filled with awe for
the beauty of every creature. There is appreciation for difference,
strength to meet adversity, joy in simply being. My dreams no longer
shriek tales of rabid fathers and forcible entrapment; they take me
now on journeys to the stars, to woodlands and weddings. This is not
to say that life does not dish up hardship and injustice. History does
not dissolve. It is only to say that I have all the resources I was meant
to have. I have become fully human.

And now, as an adult in this empire world, I am humbled again. A
most crucial mindfulness is required of me. The maps I have learned
are dangerously incomplete, the histories I have studied absurdly
one-sided. In my schooling I have been taught that imperialism is
natural, that a world made of expanding splotches of pink and mustard-yellow is progress, that the technologies required to further such

development express evolution's highest offering, that people living sustainably are laughably anachronistic. More recently, via corporate science and advertising, I have been told that the human organism is nothing more than a shave of DNA, that my yearning for community can be answered by a laptop computer, that eating a burger at the airport is culture, that corporate domination is free trade and democracy, that those who are called freedom fighters may, in the end, be terrorists and those who are called terrorists may be freedom fighters. My entire education has been shaped by the defended, and banal, projections of conquest. The task now is to expand beyond the identity and experience of the empire world. It is to learn the stories so long squelched and denied: of native peoples, the vanquished, losers in war, survivors of conquest, the *other* side of the story. The task is to realize the culture and community that have been erased: knowledge of animals and seasons, music of the land, extended family, cooperation, celebration. The task is to remember. My people. Our history. The good and the horrendous, nothing left out, colonizer and colonized indelibly intermingled, indelibly embraced.

My family tree is an elaborate set of documents, a big thick book complete with names, places, and dates of births, marriages, and deaths meandering its complex way back to the British Isles of the 1200s. I have a friend whose grandparents arrived at Ellis Island at the turn of the century and had their surname erased forever. What cannot be excavated in exactitude can be supplemented in a general way by history — by going all the way back, back through the American century, through inventions and wars, the rise of the West, back through "Long live the Queen" to our own indigenous roots. We of the empire world are caught at a fateful moment. We are asking, we are learning, digging through time and deep inside, crying, hoping, inventing. And in this process of homecoming, we are becoming fully human.

~

Listen now. Do you hear?

The Treaty of Guadalupe Hidalgo is speaking. The Treaty of Hopewell has a voice. Medicine Creek. Fort Laramie. The Northwest Ordinance. The Treaty of Dancing Rabbit Creek. They are telling us about conquest. About promises. And betrayal. About the clash, which has become archetypal, between a system hell-bent on expansion into the future and ways, far older, that derive livelihood and meaning from the ancestors and the Earth.

There is another treaty, an earlier one, and it is revealing for it actually maps out the principles of good relationship. I am drawn to this treaty because I am of Dutch ancestry, and it, the Two Row Wampum, lays the terms for peace and friendship between the Haudenosaunee (Iroquois) Confederacy and the Dutch in the 1600s. I consider it my responsibility to live up to the treaty of the Two Row Wampum.

Gather pebbles. Pick up stones.

White wampum are made of the inner whorl of the whelk shell; purple beads come from the dark eye of the quahog clam. Native peoples in North America strung wampum into necklaces and wove them into belts to record events, ideas, pledges, and treaties between political entities. The Two Row Wampum is a belt, probably two or three feet long, probably thirteen beads deep. I say "probably" because no one knows for sure where the original belt is. But to this day its legend is told and retold among the Haudenosaunee.

It is a map, they say. Two rows of purple beads are sewn side by side onto a background of white beads. The rows represent the native peoples of the lakes and woodlands, the Haudenosaunee, and the European newcomers, the Dutch. The white background is a river. Maybe it is what we call the Hudson River. Maybe it is the River of Life. The idea is that both peoples will travel along the river — the natives in their canoes, the Dutch in their "half-moon" ships — each taking responsibility for their own ways, their own governments, beliefs, and communities, living side by side in peace and friendship. The rows are equal in size, and they are parallel. One row is not bigger or longer or more ornate. The belt acknowledges that the communities are equal. Respect between them, not meddling or interference, defines the spirit of the Two Row Wampum. Interestingly, as this map of political protocol is explained by tribal elders Jacob Thomas and Huron Miller, "We will dress the same way as [when] we met so that our people will know who we are. I will put on my buckskin clothing, you will dress the same way you dressed when you first came to our people."[1] Respect for difference — in essence, sovereignty — is primary to the peace and friendship that is desired and predicted to last "as long as the sun shines upon this earth, as long as the water still flows, as long as the grass grows."[2]

Sovereignty.

Like humility, it embodies the opposite of imperialism's forceful bid. On the surface, sovereignty seems at odds with the oneness so fiercely longed for in a world scattered by empire and then (ironically) promised by global hegemony. And yet sovereignty is the quality of the day. It hovers at the horizon like a dream, existing before empire and beyond, waiting to be admitted, explored, heralded, embraced, and celebrated before any universal communion among peoples can be achieved. Sovereignty is community human-scale freedom democracy. Way back in the 1600s, the Two Row Wampum foresaw a world in which cultures would be superimposed upon each other's terrains and making decisions for other peoples would become so commonplace as to appear normal. The Two Row Wampum predicted there would be a breed of Two-Minded People who, with great hubris, would ride the waves with one foot in a canoe and one foot in a tall ship. The belt foretold that a wind would howl across the river, the water would grow choppy and cold, and the people stretched between the two rows would fall into the icy rage and drown. The alternative to the prophesy is sovereignty. It is separate rows of purple beads traveling, side by side and respectfully, down the River of Life.

OK. Now that we have established our grasp of the principles of right relationship, *now* we can tell our stories — our hurts and losses, our strengths, our joys. Now that we have shown honor. Now that we know something of the lives that unfold at the margins of empire and in its clutches. Now that we understand the distance between the colonized and the empire. And the anger. Now that we know about our own varied histories and have found strength in ourselves. Now that we understand the beads and the belt. *Now* we can work together. And on our most pressing and shared concerns: healing ourselves, resistance against domination, nurturing sustainability. *Now* we can offer our expertise — our urgency about the destruction of the environment, our ideas about organic gardening and solar energy. Now we can communicate our concerns — about the suffering rampant *within* the empire, about despair and hope, about the future of life. Now we can forge a politic that honors and connects us all.

And now, riding this pony down the mountain, through the slapping branches, as the twilight descends like a blindfold over my Dr.-Dean-Edell-+1 eyes, I am truly eating humble pie. Do I rein this way? Or that? Revert to my straight-line propensities? Or attempt to follow the curve of the land? The trail guides me for a time. Then it disappears. And then, it seems, I hope, reappears. The route has never been taken before. I could be a road namer. I could call it Horse or Pine or Down-the-Mountain — if there even *is* a road! Every cell of my body is alert.

My horse jerks back, nervous, suddenly tense. I clutch my thighs into her ribs and pull back on the leather. She relaxes for a moment and then again, in equine panic, freezes rigid beneath me. I stare into the forest. The sun is fast disappearing and the woods turning to dusk. About twenty feet to the right, I detect a large, shadowy figure. It is a bear. My horse has caught her scent, but she not ours. The bear seems about five feet tall. She is the burned color of oak brush and has a small face with a pointed snout. She is sitting up perfectly straight pawing at a dead snag lying open in the grass. She does not see us. We are pinto against the mottled palette of the woods.

I have never encountered a bear before, except of course in my childhood readings. But never in the flesh and never in her world. My mind stampedes. Bears. Do you stare them in the eye? Or look away? Freeze? Flee? Or charge?

I . . . I can't . . . remember.

And then my horse, in the chaos of her terror, slams a rock with her hoof: a metallic clap takes flight through the evening ponderosas, arriving into bear awareness in an instant. She starts.

I am suddenly paralyzed atop my paralyzed steed. Time is paralyzed. The bear studies us. And then she rises up to her full height. Uh . . . she's taller than five feet. And then, as if in slow motion, she lifts her snout into the air and tips it toward a pile of granite rocks that lie like a wall nearby. What? For all the words of instruction offered in wilderness manuals on encounters with bears, there cannot be mention of *this*. She holds the posture for a long deliberate moment, the only motion detectable this curious tipping of the snout. Then, suddenly, she drops onto all fours and takes off like a bullet.

Almost as suddenly twilight turns to darkness. Exhausted and stiff with adrenaline, I dismount and stroke my pony into ease. My blood is running ice-quick. I would have to say we are in a fix. In the wake of the bear, the woods seem unpredictable and dangerous. I drop the reins and pace the length of the horse's body. Should we . . . ? Uh . . . eh? What? For all my disorientation, I cannot dismiss the vision of the bear pointing her snout into the night. And then, guided by some strange force, as if my bones know more than my brain, I launch toward the wall of rocks. Just as Snowflake promised, the moon is ascending through the trees, and it casts its near-full illumination across my path. To my surprise, the wall is not entirely opaque. It harbors an opening like a tunnel, about ten feet deep and just wide enough for a horse with saddlebags stuffed with flowers to pass through. I lean into the shaft. On the other side, bright and silver from the moon's reflection, there is a meadow. And a trail, a recognizable trail — and it is headed in the direction of home.

Our maps to the future seem dark and unformed, like a forest at nightfall. One thing we know: we do not want any more of this conquering. Each stone we place onto our handmade maps is a nugget pointing in the direction of our ambition. It is not a known place or destination; rather it is a quality we might take with us on the journey. HUMILITY. Some of the stones are minute boulders of molten rock. RESPECT. Some are flecked with silvery mica. HEALING. Some stones are colored pink and brown like trout in the stream. PASSION. Galaxies of granite, quartz, and turquoise. RESPONSIBILITY. Some are ridged with imprints of ancient shells, revealing that they are survivors of the epoch when the desert was ocean floor. SOVEREIGNTY. Shells and buckskin. The notion bores deeper than the justice it proposes for today's native peoples. It has a universal feel. The empire world cracks open, scatters, breaks up the rocks. How did people live before imperialism? SUSTAINABILITY. Look. Homelands lie beyond the straight-line borders and Latin-Long checkerboards of nation-states. The journey to them promises to sever us from empire's perceptions and dictates. Are we ready to disembark? Ready to move toward a terrain shaped by mountains, demarcated by watersheds, populated by animals and trees, reachable only with clear sight and deep caring?

"I AM SCERCHING FOR A NEW HOUSE FOR OWL SO HAD YOU RABBIT."[3] The creatures of 100 AKER WOOD are on a similar quest. It is a quest that captures the imaginations of millions of adults and children throughout the British and American empires. I am holding my mother's tattered copy of *Winnie-the-Pooh*, the one inscribed to her from Aunt Ellen on Christmas Day, 1926. The publisher's page shows that the first edition comes out in October. By November, the thirty-ninth edition has already left the printer and arrived in Cleveland. And here too is my mother's musty copy of *The House at Pooh Corner*. It has her name scrawled HOOKR in orange Crayola on the front-inside cover. The first printing is September 1928; the thirty-fourth, September 1928. Why does it sell so wildly? Rum-tum-tum-tiddle-um. The stories are fanciful, the language inventive, the "decorations" by Ernest Shepard priceless. I am particularly enamored of the use of CAPITALS, which appear throughout like good-natured parodies of Chaucer and Milton and Shakespeare. But as Eeyore announces in a hoarse whisper, "We have been joined by something."[4] One current of literary criticism identifies deeper themes in children's stories — critiques of the British monarchy hidden within *Alice in Wonderland*, for instance. I wouldn't have seen it without Snowflake Martinez's sharp eye. The bears and donkeys and tigers and heffalumps of 100 AKER WOOD are not just from England. Like us, they hail from divergent habitats throughout the empire. Each is unique, some not even suited to the English countryside. And yet here they are, living in a land-based community (bioregional, you might venture to suggest) hunting woozles, celebrating birthdays, surviving weather, writing songs about their lives, rebuilding homes, helping each other, being irritated with each other — doing all the things our ancestors did together, in a simple way, before imperialism and the industrial revolution and the global economy disrupted our ways of life. Doing all the things the readers of England and the United States would be missing round about 1926 and 1928, one hundred years after the great garden party of empire and industrialism melded land-based communities into mass technological society.

At the end, Christopher Robin is going away. Pooh and Piglet and Rabbit cannot imagine where — off the map, for all they know — and yet we the readers know he is being sent away to school. School where he will study "People called Kings and Queens and something called Factors, and a place called Europe, and an island in the middle of the sea where no ship came, and how to make a Suction Pump (if you want to), and when Knights were Knighted, and what comes from Brazil."[5] Not how to seek out breakfast in the forest, identify animal tracks in the snow, live through rainstorms and floods, give medicine to a child, sing songs of praise and honor. No. Christopher Robin will study the knowledge of pink and mustard-yellow globalism.

Pooh is worried. He senses he will not be smart enough to understand what Christopher Robin will know when he returns. (And *this* from the bear who has written "all the Poetry of the Forest.") Christopher Robin is also upset. "Pooh," he pleads, "*promise* you won't forget about me, ever. Not even when I'm a hundred."[6]

The journey home severs us from empire's constructions of kings and suction pumps, of linear perspective and kilobits per second microwave. We make our own maps — maps not of parchment or cyberspace, but of twigs and corn husks, of shells and buckskin, of our bodies lying against the reverberations of history. Maps not of destinations, but of directions and currents, of visions and relationships. We place small stones on these maps to remind us of the strengths and awarenesses we must bring to the trek. Look at them carefully, study them, memorize. Take a full breath. Now: leave all the maps behind. We do not know precisely where we are going or how we will get there. But thank Creation, we are not alone anymore.

WE ARE HERE

Snowflake Martinez and his band of land grant heirs reach the capital on the night of the full moon. A historic bill to bring justice to land claims in New Mexico passes the United States House of Representatives in the late 1990s, but dies when the session ends and the Senate has not yet voted. The effort continues, with renewed enthusiasm. The U.S. General Accounting Office has just documented and reviewed all the claims and is making recommendations to the federal government for restitution.

Chellis Glendinning makes it down the mountain on her pinto pony. She works now for the rights of land-based cultures in New Mexico and sees this work as a vision of survival for all people.

Snowflake and Chellis still ride together, mostly in the summer, mostly to gather cota up by the Río Frijoles, always without a map.

Notes

LOCATION UNKNOWN

1. Edward Said, *Culture and Imperialism* (New York: Vintage, 1993), 5–6.

2. Print advertisement for Compaq Deskpro 386/33, 1989.

3. Said, *Culture and Imperialism*, 7.

THE MAP

1. Robert Romanyshyn, *Technology as Symptom and Dream* (London: Routledge, 1989), chapter 3.

2. Ibid., 70.

3. David Greenhood, *Mapping* (Chicago: University of Chicago Press, 1944, 1965), 128.

4. W. W. Jervis, *The World in Maps* (Oxford: Oxford University Press, 1938), 39.

5. N.F.R. Crafts, *British Economic Growth during the Industrial Revolution* (Oxford: Oxford University Press, 1985), 9–17; and Kirkpatrick Sale, *Rebels against the Future* (Reading, Mass.: Addison-Wesley, 1995), 44.

ROUTES AND ROADS

1. Donald Jackson, *Letters of the Lewis and Clark Expedition* (Urbana: University of Illinois Press, 1962), 61–66.

2. William Goetzmann, *Exploration and Empire* (Austin: Texas State Historical Association, 1966, 1993), 6–7.

3. Major General Alexander Macomb to Captain B. C. Bonneville, Washington, D.C., July 29, 1831, in Bonneville File R.G. 46,

National Archives; and Goetzmann, *Exploration and Empire*, 149.

4.   Words by Rose Bonne, music by Allen Mills. Peer International Canada, 1952.

5.   Drake Hokanson, *The Lincoln Highway* (Iowa City: University of Iowa Press, 1988), 19.

6.   John McIntyre, "Lincoln Highway," WEAF NBC Radio, Chicago, 1940; and Hokanson, *Lincoln Highway,* 129.

7.   Helen Leavitt, *Superhighway Superhoax* (New York: Doubleday, 1970), 40.

8.   Ibid., 115–16.

9.   A. Q. Mowbray, *Road to Ruin* (Philadelphia: J. B. Lippincott, 1968, 1969), 14.

THE HOUSE

1.   Ernest M. Jessop, "The Queen's Private Apartments at Windsor Castle," *Pall Mall Magazine* 18, no. 76 (August 1899): 436–49.

2.   Ibid., 439.

3.   Alfred McCoy, *The Politics of Heroin* (Brooklyn, N.Y.: Lawrence Hill Books, 1972, 1991), 4, 80.

4.   Eric Hobsbawn, *Industry and Empire: The Making of Modern English Society* (New York: Pantheon, 1968), 15, 55–56, 119, 311; and McCoy, *Politics of Heroin,* 7.

5.   U.S. Secretary of Commerce and Labor, Department of Commerce and Labor, *Statistical Abstract of the United States, 1910* (Washington, D.C.: U.S. Government Printing Office, 1911), 536–37, 540; and McCoy, *Politics of Heroin,* 7.

6.   Frank Emory Bunts, *Letters from the Asiatic Station, 1881–1883* (Cleveland: Alexander T. Bunts, 1938), 13.

7.   Ibid., 48.

8.   Howard Zinn, *A People's History of the United States, 1492–Present* (New York: Harper Perennial, 1995), 292.

9.   Charles Dickens, *Dealings with the Firm of Dombey and Son* (London: 1846); and Charles Dickens, *Dombey and Son* (Harmondsworth, England: Penguin, 1970), 50.

10. Jessop, "Queen's Private Apartments," 438.

11. Bunts, *Letters*, 24.

THE GARDEN

1. See Phyllis Dean, *The First Industrial Revolution* (Cambridge: Cambridge University Press, 1967); W. G. Hoskins, *The Making of the English Landscape* (Harmondsworth, England: Penguin, 1985); W. M. Howitt, *Rural Life in England* (London, 1838); and M. E. Turner, *English Parliamentary Enclosure* (Hamden, Conn.: Archon Books, 1980).

2. Kirkpatrick Sale, *Rebels against the Future* (Reading, Mass.: Addison-Wesley, 1995), 35.

3. Thomas Burnet, *The Sacred Theory of Earth* (London, 1684).

4. Sir John Pratt, *China and Britain* (New York: Hastings House, 1944), 28.

5. Alfred W. Crosby, *Ecological Imperialism: The Biological Expansion of Europe*, 900–1900 (Cambridge: Cambridge University Press, 1986), 149.

6. Ibid., 145.

OTHER PLACES

1. Joseph Conrad, *Heart of Darkness and the Secret Sharer* (New York: Signet, 1910, 1978), 65.

2. Samuel Eliot Morison, ed. and trans., *Journals and Other Documents on the Life and Voyages of Christopher Columbus* (New York: Heritage, 1963); and Kirkpatrick Sale, *The Conquest of Paradise* (New York: Knopf, 1990), 102.

3. Morison, *Journals,* 67; and Sale, *Conquest,* 101.

4. Morison, *Journals*; and Sale, *Conquest*, 103.

5. Morison, *Journals*; and Sale, *Conquest*, 103.

6. Morison, *Journals*; and Sale, *Conquest*, 103.

7. Morison, *Journals*; and Sale, *Conquest*, 103.

8. Morison, *Journals*; and Sale, *Conquest*, 93.

9. Morison, *Journals*; and Sale, *Conquest*, 93–94.

10. Morison, *Journals*; and Sale, *Conquest*, 96.

11. Morison, *Journals*; and Sale, *Conquest*, 100.

12. Morison, *Journals*, 212; and Sale, *Conquest*, 140.

13. Morison, *Journals*, 226; and Sale, *Conquest*, 138.

14. Nelson Lee, "Three Years among the Comanche," in *Captured by the Indians, 1750–1870*, edited by Frederick Drimmer (New York: Dover, 1961), 287.

15. James Seaver, *A Narrative of the Life of Mary Jemison* (Canandaigua, N.Y.: J. D. Bemis, 1824), 39.

16. Ibid., 64.

17. Christmas card from Randy Hutchinson to Chellis Glendinning, December 1966.

FROM DOMINION-PINK TO TOYOTA-BLUE

1. Ezra Bowen, ed., *1950–1960: This Fabulous Century* (New York: Time-Life Books, 1970), 250.

2. Eqbal Ahmed, "The Neo-Fascist States: Notes on the Patholgy of Power in the Third World," *Arab Studies Quarterly* 3, No. 2 (Spring 1981): 170-180.

3. Interview with David Musto in Alfred McCoy, *The Politics of Heroin* (Brooklyn, N.Y.: Lawrence Hill Books, 1972, 1991), 437.

4. Carlos Heredia and Mary Purcell, "Structural Adjustment and the Polarization of Mexican Society," in *The Case against the Global Economy*, edited by Jerry Mander and Edward Goldsmith (San Francisco: Sierra Club Books, 1996), 278–82.

5. Alexander Goldsmith, "The Seeds of Exploitation," in Mander and Goldsmith, *Case against the Global Economy*, 268–69.

6. Tony Clarke, "Mechanisms of Corporate Control," in Mander and Goldsmith, *Case against the Global Economy*, 298.

7. "Corporate Globalization Fact Sheet," CorpWatch (March 2001), <www.corpwatch.org>

8. Tom Barry, ed., *Mexico: A Country Guide* (Albuquerque: International Hemispheric Education Resource Center, 1992), 163.

9. Richard Rothstein, "Free Trade Scam," *L.A. Weekly*, May 17–23, 1991.

10. *New York Times*, May 12, 1991; and Richard Barnet and John Cavanagh, *Global Dreams: Imperial Corporations and the New World Order* (New York: Simon & Schuster, 1994), 238.

11. Richard Douthwaite, *The Growth Illusion* (Tulsa: Council Oak Books, 1992).

12. "Corporate Globalization Fact Sheet," CorpWatch.

13. *Washington Post*, July 1, 1993; and Barnet and Cavanagh, *Global Dreams*, 156.

14. Kai Mander and Alex Boston, "Wal-Mart: Global Retailer," in Mander and Goldsmith, *Case against the Global Economy*, 333.

15. "Corporate Globalization Fact Sheet," CorpWatch.

16. Interview with Dusty Kidd, Nike public relations, in Barnet and Cavanagh, *Global Dreams*, 326; and "Whatever Happened to the New World Order?" *24 Hours Supplement*, (February 1992), 8.

17. Gail Johnson, "Is Nike Losing Its Swoosh?" *Adbusters*, no. 19 (autumn 1997), 57.

18. United Nations Development Program, *Human Development Report, 1992* (New York: United Nations, 1992), 6.

19. David Korten, "The Limits of the Earth," *The Nation*, July 15–22, 1996, 16.

CYBER-MAP

1. Print advertisement for MCI, 1996.

BANANA-REPUBLIC SUPERHIGHWAY

1. Joseph Judge, "Where Columbus Found the New World," *National Geographic* 170, no. 5 (November 1986), 569.

2. Pablo Neruda, "United Fruit Company," in *Twentieth-Century Latin American Poetry*, edited by Stephen Tapscott (Austin: University of Texas Press, 1996), 214.

3. Michael Parenti, *Against Empire* (San Francisco: City Lights Books, 1995), 24.

4. "Highway Lets Computers Do the Driving," *New Mexican*, July 23, 1997.

SMART APARTMENT

1. Franklin Saige, "A Drive to Consume," in *Plain*, edited by Scott Savage (New York: Ballantine, 1998), 127.

2. Print advertisement for Qwest, September 1997.

3. Nicholas Negroponte, *being digital* (New York: Vintage, 1995), 6.

4. Print advertisement for Xerox, September 1997.

5. Print advertisement for AT&T, July 1996.

6. Print advertisement for Isuzu, September 1997.

7. Print advertisement for AT&T, September 1997.

8. D. A. Pollock, M. S. Rhodes, C. A. Boyle, et al., "Estimating the Number of Suicides among Vietnam Veterans," *American Journal of Psychiatry* 147 (1990): 772–76.

9. Diane Russell, *Sexual Exploitation: Rape, Child Sexual Abuse, and Sexual Harassment* (Beverly Hills: Sage, 1984), and Judith Herman, *Trauma and Recovery* (New York: Basic Books, 1992), 30.

VIRTUAL WILD

1. *Webster's Collegiate Dictionary*, 5th ed. (Springfield, Mass.: Merriam-Webster, 1943), 1122.

2. See Howard Rheingold, *Virtual Reality* (New York: Summit Books, 1991).

3. Charles Petit, "Firefly Genes Light Up Stanford Research Mice," *San Francisco Chronicle*, October 11, 1997.

4. Martha Crouch, "Biotechnology Is Not Compatible with Sustainable Agriculture," *Journal of Agricultural and Environmental Ethics* 8, no. 2 (1995), 103–4.

THE SAME PLACE

1. Denver International Airport "Visitor's Guide" and press packet, January 1995.

2. David Nicholson-Lord, "The Politics of Travel: Is Tourism Just Colonialism in Another Guise?" *The Nation*, October 6, 1997, 12.

3. Barbara Crossette, "Surprises in the Global Tourism Boom," *New York Times*, April 2, 1998.

4. Nicholson-Lord, "Politics of Travel," 14.

5. Jeff Greenwald, "Thinking Big," *Wired*, (August 1997), 99.

6. Television advertisement for Isuzu, July 1996.

THE BORDER

1. John C. Ryan and Alan Thein Durning, *Stuff: The Secret Lives of Everyday Things*, NEW Report no. 4 (Seattle: Northwest Environment Watch, January 1997), 14–19.

HOME

1. Richard Hill, "Oral Memory of the Haudenosaunee: Views of the Two Row Wampum," *Northwest Indian Quarterly* 7, no. 1 (spring 1990): 27.

2. Ibid., 26.

3. A. A. Milne, *The House at Pooh Corner* (New York: Dutton, 1928), 145.

4. Ibid., 158.

5. Ibid., 174–75.

6. Ibid., 177.

About the Author

JACK HERRERON

Chellis Glendinning has been engaged in movements for social change for more than forty years and in 2001 was named by the *Utne Reader* as one of the world's "most original thinkers." Her books include the acclaimed *My Name Is Chellis and I'm in Recovery from Western Civilization*, *When Technology Wounds*, which was nominated for a Pulitzer Prize in nonfiction; and *Waking Up in the Nuclear Age*. Glendinning is a psychologist, poet, pioneer in the field of ecopsychology, and fighter for environmental justice. She lives in the village of Chimayó in northern New Mexico.

If you have enjoyed *Off the Map*, you might also enjoy other

BOOKS TO BUILD A NEW SOCIETY

Our books provide positive solutions for people who want to make a difference. We specialize in:

**Progressive Leadership • Resistance and Community
Environment and Justice • Conscientious Commerce
Natural Building & Appropriate Technology • New Forestry
Sustainable Living • Ecological Design and Planning
Educational and Parenting Resources • Nonviolence**

New Society Publishers

ENVIRONMENTAL BENEFITS STATEMENT

New Society Publishers has chosen to produce this book on New Leaf EcoBook 100, recycled paper made with 100% post consumer waste, processed chlorine free, and old growth free.

For every 5,000 books printed, New Society saves the following resources:[1]

25	Trees
2,283	Pounds of Solid Waste
2,512	Gallons of Water
3,276	Kilowatt Hours of Electricity
4,150	Pounds of Greenhouse Gases
18	Pounds of HAPs, VOCs, and AOX Combined
6	Cubic Yards of Landfill Space

[1] Environmental benefits are calculated based on research done by the Environmental Defense Fund and other members of the Paper Task Force who study the environmental impacts of the paper industry.

For more information on this environmental benefits statement, or to inquire about environmentally friendly papers, please contact New Leaf Paper – info@newleafpaper.com Tel: 888 • 989 • 5323.

For a full list of NSP's titles, please call **1-800-567-6772** *or check out our web site at:*

www.newsociety.com

NEW SOCIETY PUBLISHERS